"In an age and culture th... voices of help and healing. Daniel and Kathy are right, of course, that good marriages don't grow on trees, but with a little help, Tarzan and Jane can make some progress."
Mark Rutland, Ph.D
President of Southeastern University

"Wow, what a great tool for building marriages! I have known Daniel and Kathy for twenty years, and their marriage and family have been a testimony to a Christian relationship exemplifying Jesus Christ. They are for real and the book is for real. It is practical and inspirational to help any couple grow in Christ and their partnership. What an asset this book is to the church and individuals who read it! Christian marriage is alive and well on the planet Earth."
Dr. Terry Teykl
President of Renewal Ministries

"I can highly endorse Daniel Bernard's new book on the topic of marriage. Daniel draws from many years of ministry experience, insights from the Word of God, and also practical points from being married for these many, many years. This book will inspire you, encourage you, and help to make your marriage strong and remain strong for years to come. Read the book. Practice the biblical concepts in it and stay on your honeymoon."
Pastor Bill Strayer
Calvary Chapel Worship Center

"Daniel and Kathy Bernard are the real deal. Their genuine and transparent approach to marriage is refreshing, practical and actually works. If you're ready to take your marriage to the next level, then you've found the right book."
Matthew Hartsfield
Van Dyke United Methodist Church

"Relationships are tough. Don't let anyone tell you different. Successful relationships take work. In a culture where so many forces are pulling people apart, I am grateful for folks like Daniel and Kathy Bernard who provide practical, biblical wisdom for succeeding in building healthy relationships. They share some wonderful principles that can help us all."

Dr. Willy Rice, Pastor
Calvary Baptist Church

"This is a very revealing discourse on the interaction between spouses. It talks about the commitment and the spiritual toughness that is needed to enjoy the blessings that God has called us to inherit as 'heirs together in the grace of life.'"

Dr. James P. Gills, MD
St. Luke Cataract & Laser Institute

"Couples are in real need of help. In Daniel & Kathy's book, *Me, Tarzan, You, Jane,* it hits the mark!"

Peter Lowe
President and CEO, Peter Lowe International

"This book is filled with practical, purposeful and passionate ways to make marriage all that it can be for a lifetime. Every couple can benefit no matter what stage their relationship is in!"

Jodie Nelson Chiricosta
Director of Outreach
Operation Blessing International

Daniel & Kathy Bernard

Evergreen
PRESS

Me Tarzan, You Jane!
by Daniel and Kathy Bernard
Copyright ©2007 Daniel and Kathy Bernard

ISBN 1-58169-233-1
For Worldwide Distribution
Printed in the U.S.A.

Evergreen Press
P.O. Box 191540Mobile, AL 36619

TABLE OF CONTENTS

DEDICATION

We dedicate this book to Kathy's mother,
Joyce Smith,
who went home to be with the Lord several
years ago. Our marriage has been the recipient
of the seeds she sowed. Her dedication as a mother
and a woman of faith has born its fruit
in Kathy's life. Kathy's strong walk
in the Lord can be credited
much to Joyce.

And to Daniel's mom,
Yvonne Bernard,
who taught him loyalty and persistence.
She tried to teach him humility, but it didn't
begin to sink in until he met Jesus.
Thanks to both for shaping our lives.

ACKNOWLEDGMENTS

Thanks to Steve and Janie Sjogren for sharing the initial idea for this book and then letting us run with it. Thanks to all who opened up their lives by writing their testimonies in this book. Thanks to Keith Carroll for his coaching and for Evergreen Press in partnering with us to publish this book.

FOREWORD

I have written the foreword to a number of books in the past several years. This one is different on many accounts. I believe this is the most important foreword of the most important book I have had anything to do with yet!

I have read many marriage books, especially books in the Christian category. Frankly, more than 90% of them have left me somewhat confused after going through them. After trudging my way through one, I have to recover after the experience. Why? For two main reasons: The first is that there is typically little room for the practical application of realistic grace—that is, presenting a picture of marriage that depends upon God's strength to survive.

Me Tarzan, You Jane! does what the vast majority of marriage books miss the mark on—this book leans into a picture of what we call a BIG GOD in order to succeed in marriage. That's why what Daniel and Kathy write about absolutely works! This is not theory—it is storytelling from decades of walking out their very public marriage.

The second reason is that once one has read through the typical marriage enhancement book, there is little life change in the end. The book you hold in your hands entices the reader to change. There is no talking down, no parental approach.

These two dear, long-term friends have helped our marriage grow stronger and deeper, and we are eternally grateful for that.

Read and soak in this message. Pass it along. Buy a handful as wedding gifts. You get the picture. This is golden stuff!

—*Steve & Janie Sjogren*

INTRODUCTION

The country was intrigued in the 1930s and early 40s with the characters of Tarzan and Jane. People thronged to movie theaters to see them, and the story lives on nearly 70 years later with updated remakes from time to time. Why not? What a story! Stranded as a boy in the jungle, Tarzan learns to adapt in order to survive. But he does far more than that for he becomes "King of the Jungle" and meets Jane, the New York City sophisticate who travels to Africa with her father and fiancé on a jungle safari.

Their story begins when Tarzan and Jane meet in the jungle, and Jane is literally swept off her feet. The intrigue was to watch these two extremely different people learn to communicate, trust, serve, and understand one another. Jane ventured into an atmosphere totally foreign to her—the jungles of Africa—with a man the likes of which she had never encountered before. Tarzan was also stepping into the unknown as he began a relationship with the first woman he had ever seen. Their life together was truly an adventure as they learned from one another. One had jungle smarts, the other street smarts. They laughed and had fun, and they were forced to overcome various obstacles and adversaries, which only drew them closer. Hold on, couldn't that description sound a lot like you and your spouse? It may be "Me Jack, You Betty" or "Me Steve, You Margie." The names and situations may be changed, but the basic story is the same.

Tarzan and Jane have remained popular throughout the years because of something far more enduring than their simple characters—the ancient art of love, as practiced between a man and a woman, that ends in a deep, committed relationship called marriage where two different people commit to venture into life together, not knowing what lies ahead.

The purpose of this book is to help couples who have agreed to face together whatever comes their way—life or death, health or sickness, riches or poverty—keep their unconditional commitment to one another. This book is not about Hollywood, but about how to overcome the real challenges that face today's marriages in our modern-day jungle.

In this book you will meet many modern-day Tarzans and Janes who are very different and know first-hand the struggles that come on the road to creating a successful marriage and family. Along with Kathy and I, they will share practical ways and helpful insights to keep your marriage vitally alive in today's jungle that threatens your love relationship. Hang on! Let's go for a swing, chapter by chapter, tree by tree.

CHAPTER 1

LET'S GET NAKED!

The characters of Tarzan and Jane—two people who came together from entirely different backgrounds—can teach us many important truths about marriage. Although they were not the perfect couple, they learned how to live together in admirable harmony.

Tarzan and Jane spent most of their married life about 2/3 naked, as was the custom in the African jungle. (In fact, in writing this book, Kathy and I decided to watch a few old Tarzan flicks. We couldn't believe our eyes that the 1939 vintage "Tarzan and His Mate" movie had a skinny dipping scene in it.) This chapter, however, is about a different kind of nakedness.

Tarzan lived the simple life of the jungle. With him, it was always "what you see is what you get." He had no time for putting on a false mask as so many of us do in modern-day life. Because of this mind-set, his relationship with Jane was an honest and transparent one.

Our goal in this chapter is to see you "get naked" or become transparent as a couple because we believe transparency is the key to positive marital transformation. A marriage is successful when a couple can be naked and unashamed not only physically, but also mentally, emotionally, and spiritually with each other.

My wife Kathy and I were about to teach on transparency at a marriage retreat being held at a resort. The session was to take place outside, close to the pool. We wrote the seminar title in big letters on an easel: "Let's Get Naked!" Unfortunately some others attending the resort took the sign literally and went skinny dipping in the pool, and security had to escort them out. Some couples are willing to quickly heed the desire to "get naked" physically, but we can almost guarantee that those same couples are hesitant when it comes to being open in their relationship with one another.

As Adam and Eve began their life together, Genesis 2:24-25 says that they were "naked and unashamed." In Genesis 3:12-13 we read of the original sin, the great fall when Adam and Eve ate the forbidden fruit. When sin entered their relationship, they became self-conscious and covered themselves. The covering was not only a physical one but a mental, emotional, and spiritual one as well.

Spiritually we find that Adam sought to hide from God. When asked about what he had done, he answered, "The women you gave me gave me the fruit and I did eat." Likewise, as Eve was confronted, she cast the blame on the serpent. This was the beginning of mankind's failure to be transparent about their mistakes. As a result, it was the first example of marital dysfunction. Unfortunately, couples have been falling into the same trap over the centuries, and we have been trying to recover from the cover-up ever since.

Can We Do It?

The means to becoming transparent is found in I John 1:7 where it says,

If we walk in the light as He is in the light, then we have fellowship with one another and the blood of Jesus covers us all.

The ability to be transparent is dependent upon our willingness to allow God's presence and light to expose our sin, weaknesses and faults for the purpose of having complete intimacy with God and one another. Jesus gives us a safety net so that we can take off the veneer of our self-consciousness with the knowledge that "the blood of Jesus covers us all." We do not need to hide any longer from God or one another. The great cover-up curse has been broken, and the blood of Jesus covers us all! Now we can have His unconditional love and forgiveness, which allows us to be real and honest—naked and transparent—with our spouse.

In the rest of the chapter we will look at the various facets of transparency—its purpose, place, problem, positive, power, plan and pleasure.

The Purpose of Transparency

The purpose of transparency is found in Malachi 2:15,

Has not the Lord made them one, In flesh and spirit they are Him, and why one? because he was seeking godly offspring. So guard yourself in your spirit and do not break faith with the wife of your youth. I hate divorce says the Lord....

In the garden, God gave Adam and Eve the command to, "Be fruitful and multiply" (Genesis 2). We are going to reproduce, but exactly what are we going to reproduce? God is seeking godly offspring. He desires we reproduce people who will reflect His likeness and character. Jesus told us to

"Go and make disciples..." (Matthew 28:19). In other words, "Go, be fruitful, and multiply." This multiplication or discipling includes not only our biological children but also others in whose lives God gives us the opportunity to invest. His goal is that godly offspring would be multiplied on the earth, giving Him glory. It is not hard to understand why He hates divorce. Divorce is the great interruption, keeping us from fulfilling our purpose and design as individuals and as a couple.

The Place of Transparency

"Where is your faith?" I protested as I continued to pound on my wife to agree to move to the inner city. She had grown up as a Christian in a suburban church, and this move would truly be a stretch for her. One morning I walked into the bedroom and Kathy said, "I need to talk with you. You are supposed to be a shepherd, but you are more like a rancher. You are driving me and not gently leading me."

She was being transparent with me, but I still resisted her. The situation came to a breaking point, and a couple in the church could see it so they encouraged us to go to a marriage encounter weekend. I still thought Kathy just lacked faith. After our first session, we went to our rooms. Again the move and Kathy's faith came into question.

"Where is my faith?" she blurted out. "How about, 'Where is your feeling?' I never said I wouldn't follow you where God was leading."

"What do you mean, sure you did!" I retorted.

"No," she said, "I asked questions and shared my concerns with you. I was trying to filter this emotionally, and you wouldn't give me a chance."

Her words pierced through my defensive shield, and I broke down and cried. I had totally misinterpreted her questions and fears. She was saying that she had concerns and emotions about the move and needed my love and patience to help her with it. It was at this point that we began a marriage of transparency.

During this stressful time, Kathy took our oldest daughter and went home to sort things out. While she was away, a new convert in our church ended up on our doorstep, upset over a broken engagement. I allowed her in and held her as she cried. Though that is all I did, I sensed the temptation to do more. She was vulnerable, and so was I. This instance could have easily gotten out of hand. Who would know that my wife was out of town for the week?

Upon Kathy's return I told her of the incident. Since then I have shared with her any time I struggle with lust. This was another place of transparency for us. (If the problem of lust is chronic, you need to be transparent with a counselor or accountability partner other than your spouse so you can deal with the root of your problem and get it resolved. Constant sharing about lust with your spouse will only bring mistrust, insecurity, and a sense of inadequacy on your partner's part.)

We need to have transparency with one another in every area and share our fears, forgiveness, and unmet needs with one another.

The Problem With Transparency

One difficulty with being transparent is that it can be painful, so we try to refrain from it to keep from hurting our spouse or feeling pain ourselves. As Proverbs states, "Faithful are the wounds of a friend." Being transparent leaves us vulnerable. When that step of being transparent is not received correctly, it is tough to attempt it again. If we stick our neck out and it is chopped off, the fear is justified. We think, "He/she will think I am silly, stupid, or overreacting. I don't want to be rejected, misunderstood or attacked, so I'll just keep it to myself." The danger of this is we become emotionally detached. We begin to grow apart or gravitate to someone else who will listen. The problem of not being transparent could bring harm and even death to a marriage.

In the following story, Jim shares that if he had been transparent with his wife he could have saved his marriage much heartache.

Shared by Jim and Elaine, married 36 years

I (Elaine) was coming off a very uplifting weekend of ministry with my church. However, my upbeat mood would soon burst. I worked as the church secretary and as usual was sifting through the weekend mail on Monday morning. Surprisingly there was a letter addressed to me from a strange woman who gave details of a relationship she had with my husband over the last nine months. I could not believe what I was reading. Surely this was a prank, I thought.

Jim and I had been married for 26 years. There was no sign of a problem. We both served God. I called Jim and told him about the letter. When he came over to the church building, he confessed that the letter was true. He had broken off the relationship just weeks before.

I (Jim) became attracted to a woman who began to pay attention to me. She complimented me and made me feel appreciated. I liked the fact that someone else could find me attractive. The excitement of having a sexual encounter with this woman was enticing. It was a big trap, and I fell for it!

If, on that first day, I would have been transparent with my temptations to Elaine, I would have avoided this snare. Since then, I have confided openly with Elaine anytime I felt tempted.

I let my guard down. After 26 years of being happily married, I never thought I'd be a candidate for an affair. I was wrong.

Elaine and I were casual about our time together in prayer prior to my fall. Sometimes it is only ten minutes, but now we daily connect with one another and the Lord. It has kept the enemy at bay in our relationship. It has created an ability to be transparent with one another. Since then, we consistently pray and spend time together in God's Word. This was one adjustment we made that was necessary to restore Elaine's trust in me.

I (Elaine) wanted to trust and see the relationship healed. I battled with thoughts of insecurity and suspicion. At times I didn't know if these were prompted by the devil or if they were emotions from being deeply wounded. Being able to freely tell Jim my thoughts and questions at any time without him becoming defensive eventually enabled me to trust him once again. Today we are back doing the Lord's work seeking to help married couples avoid the mistakes we made.

Another problem with being transparent is doing it in an uncontrolled undisciplined outburst. Blurting out how we feel in the moment without any self-control will only create a greater wedge in the relationship. If you have done this, you need to say, "I felt that way because I was hurt and frustrated, but I really don't believe that about you." Usually the damage is already done, and it will take time and positive loving and acceptance in order to build a safe place for transparency to happen again.

Andy and Jill's marriage was such a place of safety for being transparent.

Confession Defuses the Devil
Shared by Andy and Jill, married 23 years

When Andy was traveling as a major league baseball player, I began to struggle with loneliness. I was bewildered by this because we had a great marriage. I wondered why I had these feelings and where they came from. The loneliness led to thoughts of lust. I began to feel guilty and ashamed because I couldn't get rid of these thoughts. During one of my accountability times with a friend, I told her what I was going through. She advised me to tell Andy. "It will disarm the enemy from entering your thoughts," she said.

I followed her advice. When Andy came home from a road trip, I prepared a picnic and we went to a local park. I had no idea how Andy would take it. I felt so embarrassed because I thought it was usually the guy who has the problems with loneliness or lust. Andy was wonderful. He didn't read into my problem with my thought life but just took it at face value. We discussed it and prayed. I have never had this struggle again. I am so grateful that our marriage is a safe place where I can share my struggles. In doing so, we have defused the enemy's power by bringing our struggles out in the light.

Of course, there are also times when complete transparency is not appropriate. My past was a place about which my wife did not need the raw or naked truth. She knew that I had many relationships before becoming a Christian and that was sufficient for her. Sharing too many details would have caused a problem.

The "Positives" of Transparency

We need to also be transparent about the positive things we see in our mates. Phrases like, "I love this about you," "I was so proud of you when...," "You made me feel like the luckiest guy in the world," "When I saw you I thought, *God, You have blessed me with a beautiful woman.*"

Transparency can come in the way of notes or letters too. Let's face it, being transparent is difficult, and writing down your thoughts can be a step towards verbalizing yourself in an honest manner. Just remember that this does not replace communicating verbally. It's good to send a note or letter, but we need to follow it up with conversation, especially if the topic is one that needs discussing.

The Harry S. Truman Library in Independence, Missouri, has 1300 letters that the late president wrote to his wife, Bess, over the course of a half century. President Truman had a lifelong rule of writing to his wife every day they were apart. He followed this rule whenever he went away on official business or when Bess left Washington to visit her beloved Independence. It is important to note that the world's most powerful leader, dealing with other leaders around the globe daily, took the time to write a letter to his wife. Most men cannot measure up to President Truman as a letter writer, however, we can (ladies also), remember special days such as anniversaries and birthdays.

Kathy has written letters to me, sharing her deep feelings and thoughts. Here is an example of a letter she wrote me one Thanksgiving.

Dear Daniel,

Just wanted to tell you how thankful I am for you. I know what could have been if we had both allowed Satan to have his way in our lives. It is really an awful thought. What a difference God can make—the changes He can do.

I'm thankful for your love. I never (well, almost never) have to wonder if you love and cherish me. You are good (real good) at letting me know! I appreciate your thoughtfulness and tenderness. I'm thankful for your love towards our children; I know you try hard to have a relationship with each of them. It will pay well in years to come when you have good relationships with each of them. You are a good example of a husband and father I want our girls to have and I want our boys to be.

I'm thankful for how God has used us to make a difference. I pray He continues to use us. Thanks for making this a very "thankful" day for me. We have so much. We are so rich in the important things of life.

All my love, Kathy

The Power of Transparency

Second Corinthians 12:9 says, "My grace is sufficient for you, my power is made perfect in your weakness." It is in our weakness we can invite God to come and be God to us. Being transparent is to declare glaring, sometimes painful weaknesses to another. Yet in our most fragile of moments is when God shows up. God says we will experience His perfect, complete, unhindered strength. Knowing that promise is available, we should run to the place called transparency. This takes humility on both parties. God resists the proud but gives grace (His power and ability) to the humble. It takes humility to say, "Forgive me; I was wrong," but those words are extremely powerful. Matthew 18:18-20 states:

> *I tell you the truth, whatever you bind on earth will be bound in heaven, and whatever you loose on earth will be loosed in heaven. Again, I tell you that if two of you on earth agree about anything you ask for, it will be done for you by my Father in heaven. For where two or three come together in my name, there am I with them.*

Through our oneness, God says, "I'll hear your prayer. I'll be providential in your life; I am with you."

The Plan for Transparency

The following are some practical steps to take towards becoming transparent.

1. Acceptance of yourself

The process of transparency begins with ourselves. Many times we do not accept ourselves and thus we cannot fully accept someone else. God tells us that we are beautifully and wonderfully made. He accepts us for who we are, how we look, despite all our past—the good, the bad, and even the ugly. A solid relationship with God helps in accepting ourselves. If God accepts us unconditionally, we need to come to a place where we accept ourselves unconditionally as well.

2. Prayer and the Word

God is ready to listen to our heart's cry. He wants us to voice our deepest needs and concerns, our highest hopes and dreams. Be transparent before God's Word. His Word will help us make our relationship with Him solid so we can develop other solid relationships.

3. Communicate correctly

We need to remember to communicate correctly and say, "I feel..." vs. "You did..." or, "I don't feel appreciated..." or "I don't feel like I'm understood...." By communicating in this way, we don't come across as attacking our spouse. We can still express our feelings and emotions without hurtful words.

Another effective way to communicate is to use word pictures that can make our spouse understand what we are feeling. For example, you could say, "I feel like a puppy dog that has been left out in the rain." or "I feel like a locomotive train out of control."

4. Do it through letters

If it is hard to communicate initially by talking because we are too upset or can't find the right words, we can communicate transparently through a letter to our partner with the intent to communicate verbally afterwards. This gives us time to cool off if we are mad and allows us time to think before communicating.

The Pleasure of Transparency

Transparency has fringe benefits, one being great sex. Sex is an exchange of our whole selves. When we are not hiding our fears or unmet needs, we can come naked and unashamed into the bedroom. This makes for wonderful sex!

Steve and Linda's story serves as a great testimony of how transparency can provide an intimacy that will carry when circumstances keep us from enjoying the physical intimacy to which we are accustomed.

Shared by Steve and Linda, married 31 years

Good sexual intimacy is a no-brainer as far as a practical way to sustain a healthy marriage. However, the real key is the word "intimacy." Good sex is a by-product of good intimacy.

Most men think of romance as being the act of having sex, but romance to a woman is totally different. Romance is creating the atmosphere that leads up to the act. I need to get my wife mentally and emotionally prepared so she can totally and willingly give herself. Sex becomes our expression of giving ourselves to one another.

Our mental and emotional intimacy is daily; it's the love pats, kisses, caresses and verbal encouragement. Yet, those may be more frequent as we draw near the time of physical intimacy. It may start a day before or that morning. It may begin with a little tease of what to expect that night. It may be a card, phone call, an unexpected gift, or a goodbye kiss that says there is more of this coming tonight.

Atmosphere is important, so light the candles and turn off the lights. Put on slow dance, romantic music. If the kids are gone and you have a fireplace, use it as romantic setting.

We like to begin with sweet conversation. Looking into each other's eyes and appreciating one another, telling each other what we love about one another. It really communicates our love, and intercourse is the climactic expression. Then as we enjoy the after glow, there is more intimate talking and holding each other.

Our emotional and intellectual intimacy came to be more crucial then we ever anticipated in our marriage. When Linda began experiencing menopause, her sex drive sharply dropped off. Other stressful events took place in our lives, which compounded the problem. She began taking synthetic hormones, which also contributed to her loss of desire. It became very difficult for me. Yet, because of the other situation in our lives and due to the honest communication about our lack of sex, I was able to deal with it. There were even times when we could joke about it.

Sexual intercourse dropped off to once every six weeks. I didn't want to have Linda feel like she had to have intercourse if she wasn't up to it, although she did at times because she knew of my need. It was our continued intimacy—emotionally and mentally—that helped us maintain a healthy marriage during a seven-year period when great intercourse wasn't happening as frequently for us.

One day we stopped into Barnes and Noble bookstore. To Linda's surprise she found me looking at a book about sex. "Why are you looking at that?" she asked. It really dawned on her then how strong the male sex drive was and that we needed some help. Through a business associate that deals with various pharmaceuticals, we found out about natural hormones. What a God-send! These natural hormone pills not only helped with other side affects of menopause, but they also helped restore Linda's sexual desire. The other forms of intimacy and preparation are still constant with the end result that sexual intercourse is much better and much more frequent.

———•———

Rate Your Transparency Level

Let's take an honest look at ourselves and see where we need to be more transparent to lead us to a place of closeness and accountability.

___ I can share anything.
___ I can share most things.
___ I am afraid to share my greatest needs, deepest fears, and highest dreams.
___ I don't share at all at a deep level.
___ I feel like some areas are off limits to me and that hurts me.

Where do you fit on this scale? Transparency does not come easily. As with anything in a relationship, it takes commitment and work to develop a deeper level of communication, but the results are more than worth the effort.

CHAPTER 2

YOU OUGHT TO
BE COMMITTED!

Tarzan and Jane were committed to each other. Each morning they renewed their love by saying, "Tarzan loves Jane," and "Jane loves Tarzan." Even when people from outside the jungle came, bringing various enticements to Jane to leave, she kept her commitment to her man. "I belong here," she firmly declared to one and all. It would have been easy for Jane to leave the jungle and have a more comfortable life, but she stayed committed to Tarzan.

If any relationship or endeavor is to be successful, it will require a commitment on the part of all parties. Marriage especially requires that resolve. It is similar to what is said about the ham and egg breakfast: the chicken participated, but the pig was committed. Modern day relationships often have a chicken mentality in that marriage is something we contribute to or participate in but we do not totally commit to sacrificially.

The following testimonials demonstrate the type of resolve required to make a marriage work. Whether you are just beginning or are well down the road, allow them to give you the attitude of endurance that the traditional vows describe in the words, "Till death do us part."

"In Good Times and in Bad..."
Shared by Jody and Terri, married 11 years

I came home after an evening course at the community college to find my front door locked. Three hours earlier, my husband had said he was taking our 3-month-old daughter and going straight home. A familiar ball of fear began to tighten in the pit of my stomach. Jody and I had only been married six months when I had gotten pregnant and then discovered my husband's addiction to crack cocaine. The past year had consisted of several moves we made in my husband's attempt to run from his addiction.

We had recently moved back to upstate New York and rented an apartment, and things seemed to be going well. As I unlocked the door, that old fear told me that he was using drugs again. I thought about all the nights that I had walked the streets searching for him. I remembered standing in the pouring rain and begging him to come home.

When I stepped into our apartment I hoped that somehow I would be wrong. What I found was devastating. Our entertainment center was empty with the TV, VCR, and all our CDs missing. I felt used and violated. As I turned to step into the next room, I noticed the stroller standing empty in the middle of the floor. Where was my little girl? There was no way Jody could have carried all that equipment and our child. What if he'd sold her for crack? I had heard of people doing that, but never really believed it. I ran the three blocks to my friend's house, hoping my husband had enough sense to drop off our child if he was going back to drugs. She wasn't there. By this time I was frantic and called the police. Within 30 minutes they caught him stepping out of a crack house with our child. My daughter was returned to me unharmed, and my husband was taken to jail. I thought my marriage was over, but he came home a week later with a promise of attending rehabilitation.

Things got worse as we waited for inpatient treatment. I never knew what I would find when I came home. I spent most of my time feeling depressed, scared, or angry. I was constantly trying to find places to hide money, but he usually found anything I hid. I couldn't trust the one man that was supposed to protect me. Two more times I came home to find the house completely empty with everything of value gone.

For nine more years I dealt with his lies, broken promises, numerous restraining orders, and ten rehabs. Everyone told me to give up and get divorced, but I saw something in my husband that other people couldn't see. I saw the potential that God had placed in him. No matter how bad things got, I never stopped praying for him. During those years, God changed me. He taught me to rely on Him and brought me through co-dependency and healed me of depression. Jesus became my comforter and confidant. Then the day came when God asked me to let go of my husband. My daughter and I moved out two months later. I thought that my marriage was over. I had no idea it was just beginning!

When my husband lost everything, he found Jesus. Alone in jail he sincerely asked God to help him. One month later he was released and entered a discipleship program. Four months afterward, we were reunited. It hasn't been easy. The first year back together was like the first year of marriage because we didn't really know each other or know how to communicate. I was used to making all the decisions and doing everything my way. Jody didn't know how to be a father or a husband. I was busy finishing Bible School and had little time for anything else. In fact, ten months after my husband came home, he asked for a divorce.

Once again, my world felt cursed. Sometimes the pain was so bad that I begged God to let me die. It seemed like I had survived so much just to lose in the end. I knew we weren't happy, but I thought that we would stay together anyway because we were Christians. This time, I couldn't blame drugs for our problems. We did a lot of soul searching that summer. Both of us had to admit that it takes more than co-existing to make a marriage. We agreed that we didn't want a divorce, but we didn't want to be miserable together either.

We began to make small changes. First, we scheduled two date nights each month. Jody turned over all the finances to me to help me trust him. He let me pick up his paychecks so I didn't worry about whether or not he was out spending it. This was a major step for him to humble himself and realize that he had to earn my trust. It was difficult to learn how to communicate, but God is faithful to complete what He starts!

We read *The Five Love Languages* and discovered what makes each of us feel loved. Jody made a special effort to surprise me with small gifts occasionally, and I learned to compliment and encourage him. Then we started praying together in the mornings. We have since become best friends and partners. The last three years have been a time of learning to trust, forgive, and become one. Every year we attend a Family Life Weekend to Remember, which helps us to better communicate and accept each other. Through all of this, Jesus has not only drawn us closer to each other, but closer to Him. We don't just have a marriage, we now have a relationship!

"It Isn't Over Till It's Over"
Mike and Carole, married 31 years

The Hall of Fame catcher for the New York Yankees, Yogi Berra, once said, "It ain't over till it's over." That was Mike's attitude towards his marriage. The divorce papers said it was over, but Mike knew there was still hope.

Mike was an alcoholic, which was the main reason for the break-up. When Mike broke his fibula skydiving, the experience shook him up and he began to evaluate his life. The resulting commitment he made to Jesus Christ freed Mike from his addiction to alcohol.

He soon began a campaign to win back his wife and children. His wife saw the difference in Mike when he picked up the children for visitation, but years of abuse and struggle kept her skeptical. Carole finally gave Mike one chance by agreeing to a date with him. That date led to many others.

Mike made the commitment to befriend his wife, and as he did so, he began to have a spiritual impact on her. Although Carole had her own faults, his spiritual influence led her to a relationship with Jesus Christ that changed her life.

By this time, Mike and Carole were serious about reuniting. Rather than jumping back into the relationship, they entered into a six-month period of counseling. Mike continued to date Carole and they slowly rebuilt their relationship. Finally they remarried on Valentine's Day and have continued strong for 20 years in their marriage to this day.

Commit to Work at It!

A good marriage does not happen by osmosis; we must work at it just as an athlete works to keep himself fit to win a race.

In the halls of the YMCA is a sign with this acronym:

F requency

I ntensity

T ime

In order to keep your marriage FIT and your family healthy, it will take a commitment of both spouses to: 1) have frequent communication; 2) increase their intensity in intentional and purposeful direction; and 3) make time for one another. The direction will need to be planned and the plan worked. To say, "I don't have much time to give, but what I give is quality time," is often a cop out. The way to quality time is by committing to quantity time. Committing to quantity time communicates, "I love you; you are important to me."

Committed to Our Differences
Shared by Bob and Tami, married 28 years

Someone once said, "Love is an unconditional commitment to an imperfect person." We have tried to walk out an unconditional commitment toward one another, rather than declaring, "I'm committed to you if...." We say, "Even if you don't meet all my expectation, I am committed to you."

It is not easy because, like most couples, we are very different from one another. We support our commitment to one another by sharing in our differences. We do not enjoy doing the same kind of things, but rather than going off and each of us doing what we prefer to do, we share and experience things together.

For instance, Tami loves to go to art galleries and museums, which bore me to tears. I like activities such as attending ball games or going to amusement parks. Because we are committed to one another, we share in what the other enjoys rather than doing things separately. As a result, we have a deeper appreciation for one another. We have both broadened our experiences as individuals, which we would not have done outside of our commitment to one another. We have found this is an ideal way to support each other unconditionally and have become a true complement to each other.

Commit to Each Other's Personal Growth

It is important to commit to the mutual growth of each other and as a couple. As growth occurs, love deepens.

"Marriage is not an endless honeymoon, but a timeless relationship of growth that never looses the frills." That personal growth should first and foremost be to grow in God as John and Anne share.

Commitment to Continue to Discover God in Your Marriage
Shared by John and Anne, married 46 years

Our early married life was very hectic because when our fifth child was born, our oldest was still five. Later we had a sixth child. They were all very welcome because there were many miscarriages along the way. We adopted three children and then had three children naturally. It took ten years to have the children and 30 years until our nest was empty. The nest is full again now with many grandchildren.

I mention all this to say that John is especially appreciated as a husband and father. Since his law office was only ten minutes away, John was able to get home by five each evening. By that time of day, I was usually holding on by a thread. Each of us always did what we saw needed doing without discussing it. If a diaper needed changing, whoever was first aware of smelly Dave or Denise got the honor. The kitchen was cleaned by whoever was first annoyed by the mess. The lawn was John's to mow and the flowers mine to water.

When we were drowning in children and responsibilities, we made a commitment to follow the Lord. We thought we knew Him, but as we continued to grow in the Lord, we kept discovering new characteristics about Him. When our babies had asthma we learned that Jesus was a healing Lord. When we blew it with the children, we learned about His forgiveness and redemption. And so it went learning and growing in Him. Soon our God was very big!

Commitment Is a Choice
Shared by Robbie and Diana, married 8 years

Commitment is a choice, first to receive and then to give. In nearly eight years of marriage (aiming for 65+ years), my wife and I have faced a variety of circumstances that presented us with choices: either to respond in wisdom and love, or to react in pride or fear. We had a choice to either assert our "rights" during mismatched expectations with each other or to put down the gloves and allow God to work. Some character squeezing situations for us include birthing and raising five beautiful children, moving residences several times, buying and running a full-time business, facing significant medical incidents, home schooling our children, weathering financial challenges, not to mention just the daily interactions of family life. It is in both the big and little trials that our commitment is tried and choices must be made.

For me as the husband, when times are tough, when tempers flare and harsh words are spoken, when diapers need changing or food needs preparing, when cash flow is pinched and business is slacking, I am constantly brought back to reflect on what is eternally satisfying. As alluring and temporarily gratifying as it is to hastily react through spouting off flippant words or taking the easy way out by selfishly saying,

"Who cares..." ultimately there is no greater satisfaction in life than learning to love others through a committed relationship. Jesus loved us first and frees us to love. It means that I first have to accept my significance to God and then daily choose to love, care for, and belong to my wife.

I often reflect on the marriage exhortations spoken to us on our wedding day. I especially recall that in looking to the Lord Jesus for my peace, security, acceptance, and purpose, an atmosphere of freedom flows. I cherish the truth that in Him I find release from my selfish pride and learn to love. In looking to Him (and not to my wife), I release my wife from any undue pressure of trying to fulfill my needs. She experiences growing room and freedom in our relationship, and we both get to experience God's good work in our hearts. In God I am free to minister to Him and then freely give His love to her.

We made a commitment to God to love each other as long as we both shall live. Life has its ups and downs, and there are no guarantees of tomorrow's coming. Each day we are learning to choose to look to Him. He shows us our weaknesses, and then He gives us love to continue to stay committed. We belong to each other as long as we both shall live.

I hope that when we're 90 years old, my wife and I will still belong to each other. I want to be a good example of a husband by being an example of showing my commitment to honor and serve my wife. To keep this commitment, I need God and she needs Him. I appreciate the counsel and living examples of married couples older and wiser than we are that demonstrate the lifestyle commitment of looking to Jesus first and letting His love overflow to each other through life's ups and downs.

——•——

A Covenant of Commitment
Shared by Gary and Mary, married 45 years

We began getting together at school events and became high school sweethearts, dating throughout our school years. After high school, we were married in 1959 and went on to college. Our parents were not totally in favor of our marriage because of denominational differences. I was Catholic and Mary was Presbyterian, although neither of us had given our lives to the Lord.

After college we embarked on a career in the Air Force. By 1970 we had three children and although our family looked successful, our relationship was beginning to suffer. Early in 1971 we began attending a Christian charismatic home group meeting. We realized our need for the Lord, and the entire family gave our lives to the Lord. We decided to follow the Lord and to be obedient to His call.

In 1972 I received military orders to transfer to Korea without my family. I had been reading the Bible and discovered a scripture that I felt I needed to incorporate in my family before I left for overseas. As a family we proclaimed Joshua 24:15: "Choose this day, whom you will serve...as for me and my house, we will serve the Lord." As a couple we renewed our marriage vows and committed afresh to be faithful to one another, "for better for worse, until death do us part."

We also realized that our relationship needed to be built around a close relationship with the Lord. Ecclesiastes 4:9-12 says:

Two are better than one because they have a good reward for their labor. For if they fall one will lift up his companion, but woe to him who is alone when he falls, for he has no one to help him up. Again, if two lie together they will keep warm, but how can one keep warm alone? Though one may be overpowered by another, two can withstand him, and a threefold cord is not quickly broken.

We realized that the cord is our Lord: He is the center strand that makes the cord strong. As we desired to change, the Lord gave us help and direction. He guided us as we had our family Bible study and prayer time together.

Over the years we have always prayed for and with our children. The Lord has honored our family covenant and has blessed our family. All of our children are following and serving the Lord. Our newfound relationship with the Lord and our desire to walk with Him and please Him as a family keeps our marriage from ruin. As we walked with the Lord, our love for one another grew stronger. We discovered that a covenant relationship was a friendship. As we studied covenant in the Bible, we saw that God had made a covenant with Abraham and call him His friend. David and Jonathan made a covenant and became close friends. Our marriage relationship became one of close friendship. We could no longer be in competition with one another, and we began to support one another's gifts and calling. Through the years our friendship, as well as our love for one another, has increased.

———•———

Commitment to God
Shared by Jim and Heather, married 41 years

Marriage is a significant undertaking, and probably one of the greatest blessings and greatest difficulties we have in life. There are many different challenges in marriage that are much like the challenges we meet in daily life. Despite the love we share for each other, my wife and I have found our own selfishness, egotism, and self-reliance to be the biggest hindrances in our marriage. It is only when we relinquish our pride and self-reliance, and depend upon the Lord that we have a marriage with any true closeness and intimacy.

My wife and I are probably two of the most opposite personalities from two of the most opposite cultures, both with different needs. It amazes us that when we are both involved in reading the Bible and praying to God, our marriage is smoother and much easier, more open, and more loving. There is something about both spouses being surrendered to the Lord that gives a special peace and joy in a marriage. Peace has been described in 2 Peter 1 as "perfect well being, all necessary good, all spiritual prosperity, and freedom from fears and agitating passions and moral conflicts." This is the peace that the Bible wants for our marriages. To obtain this peace, we have to find ourselves totally surrendering to God, looking to Him rather than to our own selves.

Marriage, like a garden, has to be tended to if you want to enjoy the fruit and vegetables it will produce. This means it has to be fed, watered and weeded. We have to be committed to see the garden grow.

Marriage will have its share of ups and down. Turmoil is inevitable when two individuals come together. Changes in life, financial pressures, and children can take their toll. Instead of breaking the marriage apart, those circumstances can help us forge a stronger bond together, but it can only happen if we are committed to one another and to God.

Our next chapter will share many practical examples of how we can enhance our togetherness.

CHAPTER 3

YOU COMPLETE ME

Can you imagine Tarzan without Jane? That is like peanut butter without jelly, the moon without the stars, lightning and no thunder. The two just go together. One completes the other. This is how God intended it to be for us as husband and wife.

In the movie, "Jerry McGuire," the main character is a sports agent who marries his assistant out of sympathy and need. The couple was united but not unified. In one scene, Jerry and his wife are in the same elevator with a deaf couple who is communicating through sign language. "What are they saying?" asked Jerry. His wife translates the communication, "He said, 'You complete me.'"

At the end of the movie, Jerry McGuire has one of his biggest nights as a professional agent, yet discovers a void and emptiness that success could not satisfy. McGuire rushes back to the wife he has been separated from. "Tonight our little company had a very big night," Jerry excitedly explained. "But it wasn't complete, not even close, because you weren't there for me to share it with." His next statement to his wife is the clincher that reunites them as he states, "You complete me."

The book of Genesis tells us, "A man will leave his father and mother and cleave to his wife and the two shall become one flesh" (Genesis 1:28). In other words, our partner completes us.

Emerson said, "My chief want in life is to find someone who can make me do things I can." God's Word also tells us that God gave woman to be the man's helpmate. Although this definition is intended for the woman, it can also apply to the man as well. The word "helper" means to "assist another to reach complete fulfillment." You are truly one flesh united in marriage when you realize that your fulfillment and completeness can only happen together. This chapter is about things that you can do together or to one another that help complete your marriage.

For example, you can **exercise together**. Staying healthy by eating right and exercising can be a shared activity that can help the relationship as well. Have a discussion and together decide on the proper diet and the right exercises for both of you. Find what exercises you can enjoy together such as: tennis, swimming, racquetball, running, or just even walking around your neighborhood. (Of course, there are also things you can do separately, such as weight lifting or aerobic dancing, that allow your spouse to exercise in a way that benefits them the most, because you want to make sure they will be around as long as possible.)

Some of the most memorable times we have had as a couple have been in **reading to one another**. An example of this was when we were traveling and my wife read us a moving story of Bruchko, a young missionary to South America. The trials of this young man gripped us all emotionally. At times, the whole van was in tears. Sharing a good book as a couple or a family is a great way of bonding and can be used as a catalyst for some deeper conversation.

We read good books to become better gardeners, business persons, and golfers so it makes pretty good sense to read books that can help your marriage or family.

Serving others in need is another way to bond and maintain a mutual respect as you labor together. There are plenty of places to serve: in soup kitchens, with disabled children, or in evangelism outreaches, for example. Try several until you have found your passion. It creates a great challenge for each family member as well.

Having a child is one of the most special bonding opportunities a couple can experience. The husband has the opportunity to serve his wife with back rubs, walking with her for her health, or just letting her know she is beautiful during this time. (Although pregnant, a woman sometimes feels ugly and fat. She needs to know she is still desirable to her husband.) Attend Lamaze classes together, and try to be there with your wife if she has an ultrasound.

Being there for the birth itself is an unforgettable moment together. Holding her hand, giving her ice chips, helping her to stay focused with controlled breathing helps her know you are there for her. I remember leaning over to my wife while she was having a very hard contraction and saying, "I feel your pain." If she could, she would have belted me, but it made for a few laughs.

It is a good idea to **keep a journal of your marriage**. It gives you an appreciation of the growth you have experienced in the marriage and reminds you of the things you have had to overcome or endure. Hopefully, those things make the marriage stronger. Remembering what you have been through helps you tackle whatever lies ahead. It is a good idea to fill it with the good times as well. When things are going bad we have a tendency to generalize and say, "It's always..." or, "We never...." Journaling keeps the memories alive and fresh.

The following are other practical ways various couples have grown closer together.

Vacation Together
Shared by Jay and Phyl, married 25 years

The last seven years we have taken two personal vacations a year as well as a family vacation. These vacations have kept romance and passion fresh in our marriage. Just as important, it has helped us to stay friends. This past year our last child left the nest. Rather than going through an empty nest syndrome, we are having a blast. We love hanging out together. We feel like young kids and are giddy about holding hands and watching the sunset. In fact, it is better now since we learned over the years to avoid stupid stuff we used to do and say that caused hurts. Because we created an environment in which to remain friends, not just husband and wife, we are able to have spontaneous romance and passion as well.

———•———

Renew Your Vows
Shared by Brad and Becky, married 18 years

After having a difficult season in their marriage, many couples renew their vows as an occasion to reaffirm their commitment to one another. Others do it because the kids are older and they want to have a ceremony with them involved. You may want to do it to celebrate a landmark such as your 10th, 20th, or 25th anniversary. Some just like the idea and do it because they love each other.

One idea we implemented from attending a marriage seminar was to renew our wedding vows annually in front of the children. Our wedding vows are framed above our bed. We take them down and recite them as the children witness it. It is a small thing, but this is one of the best PDAs (Public Displays of Affection), I can think of. Reaffirming our love for one another has indelibly planted the joy and commitment that comes in a marriage to our children.

Laugh Together
Shared by Mike and Linda, married 17 years

After three days of constant work on our first try at remodeling our home, we both were getting irritable. Linda finished her section of painting and slumped on the couch. A few minutes later I came down off the ladder only to have Linda give me a directive while lying on her back. "You need to straighten out that line," she said pointing to the wall. How she could tell if something needed straightening or not from her position I'll never know. Up the ladder I went. When I came down from the ladder a second time, she noticed another area that needed touching up. Back up the ladder I went. Before coming down a third time I asked, "Anything else, Saheeb?" We both burst into laughter, and the tension from the day slipped away.

Laughter and a good sense of humor have always been a big part of our marriage. Linda admits that her first attraction to me was my sense of humor. Life and marriage is difficult. Keeping things light makes our life together enjoyable.

A key to a good sense of humor is timing.

Without it, attempts at being funny can backfire. Linda gets very tense before traveling. To relieve the tension, I used to cut up as we approached the time to travel, but I soon learned it only aggravated her more. There are times when kidding is not appropriate, and I needed to learn when to quit. Sometimes I get on a roll and go too far in teasing so that others feel as if I'm rolling over them. A few good pokes of fun are okay, but when I continued too long, I would hurt others' feelings.

Laughter or the lack of it has become a barometer for us. Some couples know that when they quit serving each other, like pouring each other coffee in the morning, that something is wrong. We laugh daily in the midst of most of life's situations, so when the laughter is missing we know something is off. It can mean a conflict from the previous night is not totally resolved. When the usual giggle is missing from Linda, I know she is stressed out about something inside or outside our marriage. This causes me to be sensitive to what is going on within her and to try and meet her need.

Additionally, I am a very healthy person. As the scripture says, "A merry heart acts like medicine." A good sense of humor is the reason for my health. Bob Hope was one of the funniest men ever to live, and he lived to be 100 years old. Linda knows that if I do not have the energy to be humorous, I am usually coming down with something.

Take Mini Vacations
Shared by Dale and Kay, married 40 years

I was hard at work on our first building project as a church. The men of the church and I were doing the work so the effort was all consuming. How consuming it was hit me like a ton of bricks on the day I entered the house to find Kay with the children and the suitcases packed ready for a trip to North Carolina.

"You can come with us on a vacation or we'll go alone, and we'll let you know when and if we're coming back. I'm tired of raising these children by myself!" she said.

All work and no play had made me a dull and distant dad and husband. I quickly got the message. It took me a couple of hours, but I soon had everything arranged and left with them on our first family vacation.

Working hard on our marriage means learning how to relax and have fun. Kay and I took up riding motorcycles. We take rides in the country with a picnic lunch and have even taken entire vacations on our bikes.

Make a daily decision to enjoy the time you have with your family. A mini vacation can be a day or a few hours that give you that needed break. My children needed *more time* with me *not more toys* from me. It took discipline and I had to work at it, but I have had weekly, "Whatever you want to do" dates with them as well. These were individual dates with each child to communicate to them my love and their value to me. Working at making my wife and family as my main priority is a lesson I learned well.

36

It takes time and effort to plan and budget for a vacation or to call and make reservations at a restaurant to make sure your evening isn't spoiled with a long wait. You have to take time to buy tickets to a movie or ballgame in advance. It is little work like that which made the difference and say to my family, "You're what are important to me."

Pray and Read God's Word Together
Shared by Gary and Levenna, married 28 years

We draw our strength from using the Bible as our devotional guide. We read a chapter, think it through, and read it over again. God speaks through His Word and sends healing power to our souls. We have come to agree on the ways of God with His people (otherwise known as "doctrine") in many details. There is a constant camaraderie and "insider" communication on how God deals with us and others because we see eye to eye on the pre-eminence of the Lord Jesus in all things.

Worship Together
Shared by Dick and Jackie, 45 years of marriage

The fact that we both are the children of ministers only added pressure to our young marriage. In 1958, divorce was a stigma that no minister wanted, so it was imperative for our parents that their kids stuck it out.

When we were first married, Dick was in the Air Force and I was working as a civil service legal stenographer for the 10th Air Force. Money was short and Dick worked extra jobs to make ends meet as the first of five children arrived in 16 months. We soon learned we needed to have ourselves and our children involved all the time in worship to keep our family together. I played the organ at church and Dick either played bass or was a lead singer. The Lord impressed us to teach our children to be worshippers, and we started a family group that traveled on weekends and holidays for 13 years, singing and giving family testimonies of God's saving and healing power.

Our obedience to that calling was the salvation of our marriage and our children. Traveling, worshipping, singing, playing, praying together, and going to church were the glue that continued to keep us together. We now have 17 grandchildren and all claim to know the Lord.

One other thing on an intimate note—the last thing we say at night and the first thing we say in the morning is, "I love you."

Recreation
Shared by Rich and Becky, married 17 years

The year we were married, a friend introduced us to boating. Our marriage and love of boating are still very much alive after 17 years. Now we and other experienced boaters get a chuckle watching other young couples go through what we did at their first attempts at boating. Learning how to boat can be frustrating with trailers to hitch, knots to tie, anchors to drop, steering to master, and gadgets to learn.

Boating has taught us valuable lessons on communication and teamwork, two essentials for a marriage. We learned our strengths and weaknesses. We know what to expect from one another and more importantly that we can trust each other in all situations. Boating can be dangerous, and we have had our share of scares as avid boaters. We have grown through crisis boating situations and have confidence in each other as a result.

Of course, one of the greatest things about boating is the opportunity to get away from the hustle and bustle of our lives. With our first boat, the cabin could snuggly sleep two. We had close romantic weekends, often finding a small secluded island to enjoy. Now the cabin and the family are much bigger. We enjoy nature and these little getaways regularly as a family. Recently we were floating in the Gulf of Mexico when a school of dolphins surrounded us. Both babies and adult dolphins playfully jumped and snuggled right up to our boat. Such incidents are teaching moments that will never be forgotten.

The Purpose Driven Couple

Couples need to understand that God has brought them together for a purpose bigger than themselves. We think it is a wise idea to have a mission statement as a couple. We recommend doing it before the wedding then refining it as you grow together in marriage. This statement will keep you on purpose and be used as a guide in decision making. Here is a sample purpose statement:

We are united in marriage in order to be a living demonstration of God's love as we compliment one another through our different personalities, spiritual gifts, and talents. As we combine these things to serve Jesus Christ, we are more effective for the Kingdom of God.

It is important to set goals and objectives, not only as individuals but as a couple. You need to be intentional if you are to grow personally and as a couple.

Once the vows have been spoken, it is actions that solidify a couple's commitment. As you have read, actions are often taken in small simple steps. Consider several of these ideas to implement this week. Possibly you gained some conviction that you and your spouse need to do more things together. If so, then act to bring opportunities of increased joy and love in your relationship!

CHAPTER 4

WHAT'S IN IT FOR YOU?

Serving One Another

After swinging through the trees with the greatest of
ease, Tarzan and Jane arrive at their destination. Tarzan
does a triple summersault, landing feet first on the ground.
Jane, being the city girl and not quite the trapeze artist as
Tarzan, always stops at a tree above him.

"Oh, Tarzan," she calls, and without saying another
word she dives 15 feet, landing in his outstretched arms.
This is jungle chivalry. She doesn't have to ask, "Will you
help me down?" Tarzan may not talk much and his
wardrobe could stand some improvement, but she knows he
is a gentleman and will be there for her. I guarantee you,
while the rest of the jungle sleeps, Tarzan and Jane's tree
house is alive at night.

Fellas, do your wives have to ask, "Are you going to get
the door for me?" or wonder, "Will he remember our anniversary?" Being sensitive to her is chivalry in the concrete
jungle. Like Jane, your wife will overlook most of your
shortcomings if she knows her Tarzan is a gentleman and is
there for her.

Dr. Martin Luther King Jr., once said, "Anyone can become great because anyone can serve." Jesus Christ said,

"Anyone who desires greatness must first become a servant." To echo the truths just stated, let us add that any marriage can be great because every marriage partner can serve the other. If you esteem to greatness in your marriage, you need to become a servant to your spouse.

The prevalent attitude in our world today is, "What's in it for me?" Unfortunately, this same attitude is held by the majority of people who are entering marriage. They are looking for what they can get out of the marriage rather than what they can give to their partner. This alone is the greatest reason so many marriages fail.

On July 7, 1915, President Teddy Roosevelt said, "I have a perfect horror of words that are not backed by deeds." Likewise, Jesus told us that those who are His friends follow His commandment to love one another. Those who really have a relationship with Jesus put His words into practice. In the same way, if we are to convey our love spoken through our vows on our wedding day, it must be reinforced with our deeds.

In the Tarzan movies, Tarzan was always serving Jane. He would wake her up in the morning and bring her breakfast. Any time she was in trouble she would do her "Tarzan yell," and he would be there immediately to save her. He was always there to meet her physical, emotional and mental needs.

The following couples share great examples of this servant attitude that needs to be an intrinsic part of every marriage.

Serving One Another
Shared by Tim and Teresa, married 26 years

We learned early on the importance of meeting the needs of one another and in this way creating a win-win atmosphere in our home. Our parents modeled giving and we've become givers as well. We have seen the truth in the axiom that it is more blessed to give than receive. The idea of serving each other is not to try to "one-up" our spouses but with all of our heart's desire to make their day easier or better.

One way I serve Teresa is to do some housecleaning on my day off. This involves changing a bed, deep cleaning our bathroom, and vacuuming the house. She normally does the chores on Saturday so my help makes her day off lighter and easier. Another way I serve her is to buy a small gift (flowers or candy) on no special day at all. I might write, "Happy Wednesday," or whatever day it is, or simply say, "I love you."

Teresa communicates her love to me in many kinds of service, including notes of encouragement in special places, cooking my favorite meals, or making sure I have enough shirts ironed for work. She will also use a small gift of some kind to say, "I love you!" If I happen to be out cutting the grass, she often fixes me an ice cold lemonade or brings me Gatorade. The old saying that the way to a man's heart is through his stomach does hold some truth. Coming home to a good dinner really does say something to your man about you. Know what kind of dishes are his favorite ones. Be creative in how they are presented. Candlelight dinners with him and/or the whole family can be fun.

The key here is serving by doing. We need to do whatever communicates to a spouse that he/she is the most special person on the planet.

———•———

Team Support
Shared by Gloria and Jim, married 51 years

Jim and I were married in 1953, which means we have spent 53 years together, working at making our marriage solid and secure. Our children and grand-children (26) ask us to tell them the key to making our marriage work. That is not a simple answer. I can say, however, that whoever phrased the term of having a "50/50 marriage" is wrong. At least one in the husband/wife team has to be willing to give and ask nothing in return. I am not saying one is out of the picture, just sort of in the background, sup-porting the other.

Praying for One Another

Statistics show that couples who pray and attend some form of worship service together have a higher rate of staying together.

Dr. Terry Teykl has developed an effective tool to help us to pray for our spouse. His *Keys to the Kingdom* are scrip-tures put to prayer. Forty scriptures are put on convenient business size cards attached to a key chain. Gary Herman in Lafayette, Louisiana, keeps a set on the dash of his car. Before starting the engine, he first engages in prayer for his wife using one of the keys. A sample prayer is:

Psalm 103:5 says, "The Lord fills my life with good things..." (New Living Translation). Lord, I thank you for my wife. She is your gift to me and a good thing. As she has been my blessing, I ask you to send people into her life today to refresh and encourage her.

To get your set of *Keys to the Kingdom*, contact Renewal Ministries at www.renewalministries.com.

The following is a testimony from a couple where prayer has made a difference in their relationship.

Prayer Made the Difference
Shared by Bill and Pam, married 34 years

This is a second marriage for both of us; each of our first marriages lasted seven years. Prayer has been a vital ingredient for us who have had anything but a "bed of roses" marriage to work through. Not only did this new marriage begin with three children, but it also included problems and situations that stemmed from our being previously divorced.

What is amazing to us both is that now we pray about everything, but we aren't even sure that at the beginning of our relationship we prayed about marrying each other! God was protecting us even when we were unaware of it. We didn't begin our marriage with a good prayer life, although we did pray at meal times and at bedtime. But much of the time during that evening prayer, snoring came before the "Amen"! The rest of the time we depended on our own knowledge and intellect for decisions that we had to make.

In the beginning, one of the hardest things for us as a couple was to pray together. In the natural, we are both very independent. Many of our disagreements were due to the old problem of us both thinking, "I am right and you are wrong." As we learned to increase our individual prayer life and then began praying together, we found out that during these times of disagreement, we were both wrong due to our attitudes; but when we included God, we found out that He had the solution for us! We find that all during the day we are conversing with God in giving Him thanks, praise, or asking for insight and direction both in our individual prayer lives and our times of prayer together. We found that there was power in agreement as we prayed specifically for concerns we had.

There have been times when, in the natural, we couldn't stand each other. That seems so hard to believe when things are going well and we feel that we don't know how we could live without each other. We have found that God can replace bad feelings with good ones. He can replace hate with love. Nothing is impossible for Him! Looking back over those low times in our marriage, we don't know how we would have made it without the power of God and the power of prayer in our marriage.

Communicating through prayer is important. Prayer is a two-way conversation—us talking to God and God speaking to us. We must learn to hear His voice. This comes through practice. When we pray, we are including God in our lives and acknowledging that He is our source of everything that we need. He anxiously awaits our opening up to Him so that He can give us the guidance, healing, wisdom, direction, mercy, and patience that we need.

Ministering to Others Through Giving
Shared by Vaughn and Narlene, married 24 years

My husband has always had a big heart, but he was actually endowed with the spiritual gift of giving about 15-18 years into our marriage. For the first five years, neither one of us was saved. My husband was always willing to try to help anyone or co-sign on a loan for any friend or relative. This willingness to help became even more pronounced after we were saved, and it eventually got downright ridiculous. The man gives *everything* away. Now, most wives I know don't have a major problem with their husband helping others, but when he starts giving while your own family has needs, things can get very sticky.

We went through some very financially trying times in our marriage, just like most young couples. Even though we were financially strained, my husband would always want to give. At one point he didn't even have a regular source of income for over a year, but he was always serving others, doing for others, and giving away whatever we had.

I remember specifically when I began to learn to cope with this. When we had been married about six years, an old mangy dog started coming around our house. I would always try to shoo the dog away, but my husband would always feed him. One day I asked him why he was feeding that old mangy dog, and with a glitter in his eyes he said something like, "God cares about everybody and you never know who you're helping." That thought really stuck with me. It was as if God was preparing me for what he would be doing through my husband later on. From that day forward, I did not question my husband's giving. I had to learn to trust God and believe that he was working through my husband to give away my wedding bands, computers, automobiles, and houses...even during times when I thought we had nothing or that we could not afford it. God has proven Himself so faithful. I know that if I had simply looked in the natural and responded in the natural, it would have put a tremendous stress on our marriage.

Financial pressure and stress has been the downfall for so many marriages. But my husband has truly taught me to not set my affections on this earth's treasures. I love him even more for showing me Jesus through his giving. I would encourage all wives to allow their husband to lead, especially in the area of helping others and giving to others...you never know whom you might be blessing.

Find Things to Smile About
Shared by Roy and Robyn, married 17 years

In marriage, we come to know our partner's weaknesses and peculiarities. It's very easy to become irritated with certain things he or she may do. One of the keys to staying power is to look for the things your partner does that you like, such as a smile, and to overlook the negatives.

For example, my precious wife, Robyn, suffered what the medical profession called a "mild stroke" a few years ago. Thank God, she's still able to carry on and live her life, not like before, but she does very well. However, the stroke affected her vision, balance, and even her ability to grip things properly. So, it's not unusual to hear things falling to the floor or getting knocked over wherever Robyn happens to be. I do a lot of work from home and sometimes, I have to admit, it's irritating to hear all the crashes. Some days, my first response is to frown and say something like, "Honey, be more careful...or pay more attention to what you're doing...slow down, or concentrate more." But I usually stop myself and go see if she's okay and then we laugh about her "accident." I just smile to myself and thank God that I have a wife that keeps on trying to keep things clean and nice. She still cleans, dusts, and decorates our place so that it looks and feels good! I don't want to frown at her. I want to smile!

———•———

Singing Through Your Sorrow

Recently a friend wrote about the joy he and his wife were able to experience even while going through the agony of losing a beloved daughter to cancer. He said,

My lady and I sing. I love singing hymns about the wondrous love of Jesus. They express what must be a common sentiment to those of us who have been "surprised by joy." Since I wrote this, we have had a severe test, but we have kept singing through it all. My lady kept singing as long as she had breath.

———•———

Sacrifice
Shared by Jay and Elizabeth, married 24 years

In one word, we believe the key to our long marriage is "sacrifice." We have learned that being selfish and demanding one's own way only leads to deeper problems. We need to step back and analyze our own selfish motives and put the other person's needs first. We also know that it was our commitment from the start to follow God together and to rely on Him, which has gotten us through tough times as well as the easier ones. He has been faithful to us, even when we weren't faithful.

Although the road is sometimes rough, having a good "traveling buddy" shows us what God meant when He said, "It is not good for man to be alone. I will make a help-mate suitable for him."

Small Deeds

In the 1942 movie, "Tarzan Finds a Son," Jane is getting breakfast for Tarzan and their son, who was creatively named, Boy. Jane turns from her kitchen duties to face Tarzan. Tarzan with a boyish grin on his face is hiding an orchid behind his back. Tarzan puts the orchid in Jane's hair and asks, "Does Jane like Tarzan?" Tarzan is one smooth operator. As you would expect, Jane has an affirmative answer: "What woman wouldn't like a man who would pick an orchid for her in the morning?" Men, what woman wouldn't like a man who did such things? The answer is 99.999% of women will love you for it.

One of my favorite sayings is, "Small deeds done with great love will make a great marriage." Here are two more ways to serve your spouse. First, give her the last piece of the pie. Men can display chivalry today without putting down their coat over a puddle of water for their lady to walk on. Don't say, "Hey, honey, do you want the last piece of pie?" She knows you are asking in order to free it up for yourself. Take that last piece, put it on a plate, add some whipped cream or ice cream and give it to her. It is showing God's love in a practical and small sacrificial way to your wife with no strings attached. When women have husbands who will make sacrifices for them, it makes it easier for the wives to love and follow them. Wives can do the same as well.

Another idea of special service is breakfast in bed. Either partner can do this for the other. Men especially could make it a special treat for their wives since their wives are the ones who usually do the cooking. You can even do this for your children. On the day you celebrate their birthday or some other occasion, start their special day off with breakfast in bed.

Unselfish Giving
Shared by Mike and Holly, married 28 years

Marriages work better when there are lots of giving and unselfish acts during the course of one's marriage. When our first son was only a few weeks old and very colicky, I was completely worn out one afternoon. Mike came to me and said, "Let me take care of him for a while. You go take a nap. We're a team." I was astonished. Those last three words gave me hope for the future with a sweet but fussy baby. Years later our family grew to include four boys.

December 26th is the best (cheapest) day for shopping so one year Mike woke me up early that day, handed me a wad of money and led me out to the car, which he had heated for me on the cold morning. He put a cup of hot chocolate in my hand and said, "Have fun, there's no hurry." Off I went to a total stress-free shopping spree, something that doesn't often happen with a family of six. These are just two of many examples of how unselfish giving went a long way in our marriage and encouraged me in raising four rambunctious boys.

Doing the Little Things
Shared by Bob and Kris, married 14 years

One way to a sustained healthy marriage is by sharing encouragement. We have been married for more than 13 years and are both professional people going a zillion miles an hour. We feel the pressures of business, household, marriage, and trying to raise Christian, value-minded daughters. We watch many couples stop talking or even start blaming each other during troubled times. An honest, yet well-timed compliment or a sincere thank you for something that is usually taken for granted can go a long way.

One sure way I have found to relieve my wife's stress is through foot massage. The dividends from spending 10 minutes rubbing her heels, arches, and toes at the end of a long day are too numerous to mention. Those ten minutes also are a time for us to really talk and more importantly listen to each other. There seldom is heard a discouraging word during foot massage time.

We also enjoy taking short vacations alone and try to have a weekly date night. We love our children, but when they are with us we can never truly focus on each other. The Good Book says to encourage one another in your day—do it and have fun!

Ways to Think of Your Spouse

Tony Compollo was speaking at a liberal college with predominantly women present. He told a story of a couple who had been out walking in their garden when the wife suffered a heart attack. She was rushed to the hospital, but she died soon after arrival. The children gathered around to comfort their father. He told them, "No, it's OK. It's a good thing that she went first." "How's that?" they asked. "It would have been too difficult for her to face life alone without me. It is a good thing that she didn't have to face that trauma." Now that is a different way of looking at the issue of sacrifice and thinking of the other person. The natural response would be for him to feel sorry that he was alone, but in this instance the man felt that it was better that he would suffer that fate than his wife.

Thinking of your spouse before they are gone is a way of enhancing and maintaining your marriage. Sometimes the problem is that we lack ideas to get us going. Here are a few to get you started:

Bring breakfast in bed	Buy his/her favorite book
Buy his/her favorite movie	Give a foot rub or back rub
Take a walk together	Plan an afternoon out
Give a foot rub	Buy an outfit
Give a spa gift certificate	Night out with friends
Write a poem	Cook his/her favorite dinner
Buy him tickets for ballgame	Go out for dessert
Have a night at the movies	Plan an overnight getaway
Go shopping together	Bring home flowers
Have a date night	Spend time on a mutual hobby
Give undivided attention for 30 minutes to share your heart	

You can even make "care coupons" for these ideas to give to your spouse for birthdays, holidays, or just because, and then your spouse can use them whenever they want. Remember, think and act while your spouse is still here to enjoy it. Live with no regrets and make lasting memories.

CHAPTER 5

FRESH BREATH

When we wake up each morning, we usually have that awful morning breath. Before we kiss or communicate with our mate, most often we try to use mouthwash or brush our teeth first. In the same way we need to make our communication to one another like clean, fresh breath.

I think someone once said (and if they didn't, I'm saying it now), "What breathing is to the body, communication is to the marriage." The following anecdote is a fun poke at miscommunication.

A woman went to a lawyer and said she wanted a divorce. The lawyer proceeded to ask her questions.

"Do you have any grounds?" he inquired.

"Oh, yes" she replied, "About three-quarters of an acre."

"Do you have a grudge?"

"No," the woman answered quickly. "But we do have a lovely carport."

Again the lawyer paused and then asked, "Does he beat you up?"

"No, I get up before he does every morning," the woman reported.

Finally, the lawyer blurted out, "Lady, why do you want to divorce your husband?"

"It's because," she explained, "that man can't carry on an intelligent conversation."

All joking aside, carrying on an intelligent conversation is a vital key to a successful marriage.

Ladies, let's face it, we are totally different than our husbands. Can any of you relate to Tarzan and Jane and their extremely different backgrounds, which could have made it almost impossible to communicate well? At first they didn't even have a common language, but they didn't let that fact stop them.

The following communication practices will open new doors to your relationship.

Magic Phrases

When I was 23 years old and becoming serious about marriage, I asked my pastor for some advice.

He said, "Learn to swallow."

"Learn to swallow! What does that mean?"

"Learn to swallow your pride and admit you are wrong because you will be, and you'll save your marriage by humbly admitting it," he answered.

Good advice! I thank God I never had to use it. (Just kidding....) "I was wrong" is one of the four magical phases to sustain your marriage. The others are, "I am sorry," "Will you forgive me?" and of course, "I love you."

I told my wife that I am excited about making love to her for the rest of my life. Good juicy stuff like that tells her, "You're mine; I'm yours and loving it." It says, "You're safe, secure, my beauty forever." Women can do the same in affirming their husbands. Your spouse needs to know that they are special, one-of-a-kind, and that you need and appreciate them.

Murdering Your Marriage

Thousands of couples poison and ultimately murder their marriage through criticism. A study of more than 100 couples who experienced marital problems showed that, in every case, criticism was a major factor. And in more than half the cases, both partners were highly critical of the other.

Criticism can put fear in your mate, and fear stifles love and affection. Criticism can cripple communication, which is the lifeline to a healthy marriage. No one ever built a monument to a critic. No one can build a healthy marriage on criticism.

Sol and Terri give good advice as to how to communicate properly and keep from murdering your marriage.

Never Use "Never"
Shared by Sol and Terri, married 13 years

Terri and I have had relatively few major fights in our 13 years of marriage, and the main reason is the way we communicate. I've learned to use the "I" message rather than "you." I'm better off saying, "I'm disappointed" or "I'm feeling frustrated" rather than saying, "You did this to me," or "You let me down," or "You made me mad."

Stay away from phrases like "You never," and "I always" in communicating. They have an accusatory tone and will only cause your partner to become defensive. You want to express your feelings without being accusatory or critical. You want the lines of communication to stay open and not slam shut because of defensive reactions.

———•◦•———

Accepting Your Partner as They Are

After the honeymoon, we find many little idiosyncrasies in our partners that are annoying. Some of these may never change. It is interesting to listen to people after they have lost their loved ones. They laugh amidst their tears and say, "I'll even miss the way he used to do that annoying...." Our idiosyncrasies make us unique even though they test the love of our spouse. This is what makes marriage so wonderful. You can let down your guard, be vulnerable, and share all your fears and intimate thoughts and hopes, knowing they are safe and you are unconditionally accepted.

After a hard day's work in the concrete jungle, there is a tendency to unload on your husband with all the details of the day. (This is also true if you are a stay-at-home mom and have been devoid of adult conversation all day.) Give him some space to unwind when he gets home. Ask when would be a good time to go over some things. Some couples set a time after supper so conversation can center on how each other and family members are doing first before attacking schedules and things to do.

Forgiveness

Forgiveness is absolutely mandatory in maintaining a healthy marriage relationship. It ties into having realistic expectations of our spouses since so many times, we expect more of them than anybody else. Learning to forgive quickly and completely with God's help is essential in building a good relationship.

Forgiveness is giving up the right to hurt someone who hurt you. Truly forgiving another means not to bring it up again. Our greatest example of forgiveness is God's forgiveness toward us.

Our daughters, Bethany and Faith, sing a song they wrote for their CD, "You Give Me Life," entitled *Unseen*

Scars. The song shares their personal experience of being hurt and learning to forgive. (To listen to the song, go to www.consumedmusic.com)

The next couple shares how they have applied forgiveness to their relationship.

Shared by Chris and Michelle, married 16 years

There have been many wonderful blessings in our marriage that have helped keep us together, not the least of which is the consistent understanding we offer each other when we're going through a tough issue. We have always been concerned with being sensitive to the other's needs whether they're emotional, physical, or spiritual. When we are not concerned or sensitive, we try to make amends as quickly as possible. We maintain a full apology system with each other and in our household by saying, "Honey, I'm sorry for this specific behavior. I really did not mean to hurt you. Will you please forgive me?" We offer each other forgiveness, sometimes after discussion, but always quickly after the apology. This allows us to never "let the sun go down" without addressing a hurt or resentment. By forgiving each other, we always draw closer together.

Develop Listening Ears

Listening is profound. I have often appreciated the wisdom my wife has exhibited in the times when I am venting my frustrations. She doesn't offer me a quick fix idea at those times or tell me that I shouldn't feel that way. She just listens and lets me vent. She lets me know that she heard me and is praying for me. Many times I just need her to be my sounding board.

Men, listening to your wife will make a profound impact on her and tell her that you really care. Women love the details, while most men do not. When she shares something with you, really listening to all the details (although she knows you don't really enjoy hearing them) makes her feel important. The fact of the matter is a wife plays a vital role because men can get into major trouble by not paying attention to the details. When this happens, we snap at our wives, "Why didn't you tell me?" "I tried, but you weren't listening" is the usual response.

Equally important is listening to your children. Has your child ever said to you, "You're always too busy!" or ask, "Did you hear me?" Those are signals letting us know we are not listening to them. Sometimes we get so busy and preoccupied with life that we do not hear what they are saying. Take time to acknowledge your child by personal attention (eye level conversation, hugs, walks) and do not use the time for lecturing and talking yourself. Listen to them, and they will share their thoughts and concerns with you. By listening, you will know them better and be able to meet their needs.

Stress Free Driving

One of the most stressful and frustrating times for a couple or family is driving, especially in heavy traffic. Driving too close, too fast, recklessly, or aggressively can frighten and stress those in the vehicle. Stress can also be added by talking on the cell phone or having other distractions in the car. Adjust your driving and be sensitive to what causes stress in your spouse or family members. Lacking this sensitivity can cause arguments and fights long after the trip is over. This is a good idea not only for physical safety but also for the emotional and mental health of your relationships.

At the same time do not be a back seat driver and overly critical of others' driving habits if they are not doing something that puts people in danger. This can hurt the relationship especially when things are not going great, so sensitivity in this area is a way of communicating love and concern. We need to drive in such a way as to put others at ease. We are carrying precious cargo, our family, and we need to be careful with them.

Public Support

Never put your partner down, especially in front of company or in public, even if it is a "joke." It can really wound a relationship. Proudly introduce your spouse. An introduction can speak volumes of your love and respect for your spouse. You can always say, "Let me introduce you to my beautiful wife..." or "...my better half..." or "...the best thing that ever happened to me."

Have Good, Clean Fights

The saying, "No hitting below the belt" is good advice for marriage. It is important to have good clean fights. Saying things about one's physical makeup or other areas that they cannot change is cruel.

However, it is healthy to disagree and have some spats. If it's done right and not too often, it can help build and not tear down the relationship. Consistent communication will help there to be less fights or disagreements. Center on the issue of the disagreement and do not personally attack your spouse.

Fight Fair
Shared by Alan and Jule, married 15 years

One of the best wedding gifts we received was in

the form of wise counsel from our pastor. During our wedding ceremony, he instructed us, "Don't sweep things under the rug and give the devil a foothold." Of course on that beautiful day amidst the romance, we could never have imagined how valuable that gift was. Thank God that we have been able to hear those words time and again on the video of our wedding.

While Alan and I didn't go into our marriage with blinders on, we had no idea of the trials that lay before us. However, one of the best things that we had going for us as we started our marriage together was our communication skills. We knew the dos and don'ts of communication. The test came in putting it into practice.

As our marriage moved forward, it didn't take us long to see that Alan and I are about as opposite as you can get in so many ways. He tends to be a risk taker, works best under pressure, and has a very black and white way of looking at things. I, on the other hand, prefer to play it safe, plan things out so that stress is minimized, and operate mostly from a merciful point of view. He was loose with his finances, and I held on too tightly. He drives in the fast lane; I prefer the slow lane. What challenges we faced! Add the stresses and tragedies of life to that, and you have a real pressure cooker!

Opportunities for horrific arguments abounded during our first years of marriage, and we took them. What we had to learn was how to take the advice our pastor had given us and apply it to our marriage. We couldn't afford to let things build up and explode, but we didn't want to nit-pick each other to death over trivial details. We began to ask ourselves what issues would matter in the future. We soon found that when we tried to resolve conflict, the communication skills we had learned were tough to put into practice.

We started to look at each other not as opposites, but as the complementary person God had chosen for us, a true gift. We realized that conflict is God's way of polishing us. That approach has allowed both of us to become more centered in our personalities and choices. We have endeavored not to use words like "always" and "never" in our arguments, and we point it out to each other if that starts to happen. We have learned not to be so quick to criticize the other person's feelings. Feelings are what they are, right or wrong, and we need to deal with them together. (A helpful book on dealing with conflict is *Fight Fair* by Tim and Joy Downs from Moody Publishers.)

The "D" Word

Don't use the "D" word—DIVORCE. Life and death are in the tongue. Speak life to your mate and into your marriage. The Bible is filled with words of life, love, and fulfillment. Dr. Sorsen of Princeton University discovered that the divorce rate of couples who read the Bible daily is one out of 1,052! When you both speak His Word, there is no room for divorce, which He hates (see Malachi 2:16). Make a commitment from the beginning of your marriage that when problems arise, you will find solutions and options, but divorce is not one of them. This forces you to work out the problems and not try to escape the relationship.

There once was a woman who wanted to divorce her husband. She went to her pastor to complain and he gave her this advice: "Serve him, cook and clean for him, rub his back, etc. He will be so dependent on you after six months it will crush him if you divorce." Six months went by and the pastor asked her, "Are you ready for that divorce?" "Divorce? No way, I love him," she said. I'm not sure who said this wise saying but it is so true: "If you will act the way you wished you felt, eventually you'll feel the way you act."

It's Better to Give Than Receive

Communicating with one another on sex is important. What your mate likes and dislikes will make a difference in satisfying love making for both of you. Communication begins with an attitude that seeks to please the partner and not just oneself. Learning what the spouse enjoys can give the most pleasurable experiences to a couple. It is better to give than receive!

Words of Encouragement

Another area that couples need to focus on is building up the body of Christ, and the first one we are to build up is our spouse and family members. I try to look for ways to compliment and encourage my wife through words of affirmation, acts of service, and hugs. One of my favorite scriptures that helps keep me focused on building up my wife or family member is Colossians 4:6 that says,

Let your conversation always be full of grace, seasoned with salt, so that you may know how to answer everyone.

There is nothing greater than words of encouragement to your spouse because they knit your hearts closer together. Our dear friends, Randy and Peggy, give two great ways to communicate encouragement.

Phone Calls and Notes
Shared by Randy and Peggy, married 24 years

Most of the time, when my husband, Randy, calls home during the day, he's calling for a specific reason or because he needs me to do something for him. Because of that, I love it when he calls for no other reason than to just say, "Honey, I was just thinking of you and I love you." That's when I usually tease him and ask, "What did you really call for?" and if he answers, "No, I just wanted to say I love you," then I walk around like a teenager in love, thinking about him the rest of the day.

One unique way my wife, Peggy, has used to kindle a little passion in our marriage actually happens when we're apart. Many times when I've gone away on a two or three-night trip, she has stealthily inserted a love note for each day that we are separated. Each envelope is labeled with the day of the week that I am supposed to open it. Every message is a note indicating how much she is missing me and how wonderful it will be when we are reunited. Let's just say that it makes the homecoming something to be anticipated. Of course I call each day to tell her how things are going, that I love and miss her, that I loved her notes, and that I can't wait to get home.

———•———

Shared by Van and Charlotte, married 30 years

The other night Charlotte and I had a falling out. As I was about to get in bed, I saw a card on my pillow with the words, "I love you" printed across it. As an added touch, Charlotte had made an imprint with her lips at the bottom. To say the least, the friction and chill left, and the flames of romance flickered again. This is one example of the timely impromptu notewriting my wife has done throughout our marriage. As we both work in our real estate company, the busy pace could cause us to lose perspective. Charlotte's writing of notes affirms to me her love and how we feel for one another.

———•———

As a side note: Keep the cards! I used to think it was a woman's thing to keep the cards and notes. I wished I would have kept all of hers and the children's. What great memories I threw away. I'm saving them from here on in. Going the extra mile to communicate for the health of your marriage is worth it. You will personally grow because of it and never regret it.

Men, maybe you feel it's easier to talk in just a few words like Tarzan when you communicate. Andy felt awkward in communicating initially, but with effort he grew in this area.

Shared by Andy and Jill, married 23 years

Jill is talker and I'm more of the quiet type. This posed a bit of a problem at the outset of our relationship. Jill would assume my silence was an indication that something was wrong. This problem was compounded by the fact that I was on the road so much since I was a major league baseball player for eight years. Even as a married man, the temptations that go along with professional sports are many. Jill needed the feedback to give her a level of trust while I was on the road, but also as an enhancer of our relationship. In other words, she needed for me to share with her on an equal level of intimacy and depth. Rather than saying, "Well, that's not me," I endeavored to go outside my character and develop better daily communication. We began letting each other know how things were going. We shared what we were thinking and feeling. As a result, we have great interpersonal communication now. Taking a daily personal inventory together not only keeps us from temptation but also enhances our mental, emotional, spiritual, and physical relationships.

Learning to Dialogue
Robbie and Diana, married 8 years

What do you do when there are differing expectations or hurt feelings in the relationship? We quickly stop, clarify, forgive, and move on, letting go of the conflict right then. That happens most of the time, but on occasions when emotions run deep, we truly have to make more of an effort to not let issues roll on. We have to recall our commitment to each other and remember the preciousness of the other as we determine to move through the issue.

One place we try to start is by keeping to simple rules of honor and dignity. "Cheap shot" words and slinging around past offenses are not allowed. We want to keep to the issue at hand and not intermingle non-related issues or a week's worth of hurts in one outburst. We have taken time in the past to learn each other's personality styles and the differences of how we respond to conflict. My wife usually reacts quickly, but to resolve a serious conflict, she likes to ponder some about it before responding. I like to fix it right way. We both have to meet in the middle and make sure we clarify what we were feeling as a result of some action or words spoken and then listen to the other's perception of it.

As we dialogue, we have to recall that we are committed to each other's spiritual success as Christians and that we should not aim to tear down the other. Thus, as our feelings are shared about the issues, we let go of any motives or actions that attempt to hurt the other. When we fall short in this process, we must simply go back to the Lord and let Him forgive us, change our hearts, and move on with us as we grow and are renewed.

The Fairness Factor

Greg Johnson, in his book, *We're Finally Alone, Now What Do We Do?*[1] helps couples learn how to dialogue.

The key to a thriving marriage isn't occasional great sex, cruises, meals out, or time away from the kids. It's the communication that occurs during those precious few moments when you can look into each other's eyes and attempt to connect.

Many times communication is tough because it is hard to initiate. What do I say? How can I get my spouse to talk to me? Mr. Johnson helps by giving questions that a couple can go through. They are grouped in five sections according to their depth of intimacy. The goal of the couple is to move on to each new level when they are ready to go deeper in your communication. Here are two examples from each level to show the various levels of communication:

LEVEL 1: What are the three best memories you have of us together before we were married? Or, when you're day-dreaming, what things do you imagine yourself doing?

LEVEL 2: Do I sometimes make a joke out of things you don't think are funny? How much does that bother you? Would you like me to change? Or, what would you like to do that we're unable to do now due to lack of money, time or ability? How can we dream together in that direction?

LEVEL 3: Is sex helpful, comforting, difficult, or anxiety producing for you when you are under stress at work? When you're grieving? Sad? How can our intimacy at those times be at its best? Or, do you ever sense that I sometimes put conditions on my love and affection for you? When do you feel the most insecure about my love?

LEVEL 4: Is there any emotional baggage we've brought to our marriage that needs to be unpacked? Do you think the process will require professional help? Or, what three things can we start doing to become better friends?

LEVEL 5: Do we honor God with the way we spend, give, and save our money? How could we do better? Or, what is the difference between emotional intimacy and physical intimacy? Which do we share more of?

One final thought, to stay alive you have to be addicted to breathing. To keep your marriage alive, you need to get addicted to communication—the breath of your marriage. Real communication can only take place as we are willing to be honest and transparent with one another. And good communication can keep the fires of romance burning, the topic of our next chapter.

[1] Johnson, Greg, *We're Finally Alone, Now What Do We Do?*

CHAPTER 6

KEEP THE FIRE BURNING

Remember in the Tarzan movies how Tarzan was always on the move to defend or rescue his love? He would wrestle a boa constrictor or alligator, swim rivers, dive off high cliffs, dodge poisonous darts, stop the evil white hunter, or swing through the jungles for miles just to save his beauty. She was put on a pedestal or at least the top tree house in Tarzan's mind. And, in turn, Jane let him know, "You're my man, my hero. I'll go with you wherever you want to go." When you have that mental image, it doesn't take much to get the flames of love burning bright.

The old campfire song, "It only takes a spark to keep a fire burning," is a truism for marriage. Small sparks keep the fires of romance burning in our relationship.

Our friend and marriage counselor, David Clark in his book, *Men Are Clams, Women Are Crowbars*, gives several sparks or acts that when applied will keep the flames burning.

Hold Hands

When you're walking together, hold hands. That's what sweethearts do! I can't believe the number of

couples I see walking along with no contact! Their
hands are just swinging free. No! Not a good idea.
What do you think your hands are for? God didn't
give us waffle irons at the end of our arms. Two
hands fit together real nice. So, hold hands! (*Men
Are Clams*, p. 206).

Real Kissing

You know what I mean. Long, involved, somewhat wet, heartfelt smackers. Sucky face! I'm
talking about open mouth kissing. Kissing with a
punch!

Stop giving each other those pathetic little
pecks! "See you tonight"...peck. "Have a nice day,
honey"...peck. "Welcome home"...peck. Two sets
of bone-dry lips touching for a millisecond. The
peck is so fast the human eye can barely pick it up.
Why do you even bother? You might as well shake
hands.

The poofy-lip kiss is another miserable excuse
for a kiss. Here, the lips are bunched together and
shoved out an inch or more from the mouth. It's as
if the kisser wants to keep the "kissee" as far away as
possible. My research shows this is the kind of kiss
eighty-year-old great-grandmothers give their great-
grandchildren.

We also have the sound-effect kiss. In this ludi-
crous scenario, the kisser doesn't even deign to
touch the lips of the spouse. The kisser just makes
the sound of a kiss and walks off! This one's a real
mystery to me. Why would you make a kissing
sound when the person is right there with you? Why
not just kiss the person?

These three kisses have absolutely no place in a marriage. Why, they are not kisses at all! You might as well be kissing the wall. It's about as exciting. Are you kissing your Aunt Sarah? No! You're kissing your beloved marriage partner. Your lover! Your soul mate. Your precious sweetheart. To give anything less than your best, top quality kisses is an insult to your spouse and your marriage. It's an outrage! It needs to stop!

It's no surprise to me that God's book on physical love in marriage begins with kissing. Very often, kissing starts off the whole chain of physical affection.

If you can't kiss properly, you can't do anything else! You aren't going anywhere else in the physical area. You're stopped at the door and can't fully explore the wonderful pleasures God has for you in physical intimacy.

Song of Solomon 4:11 (NAS) is probably the greatest, most explicit verse in the Bible about kissing:

Your lips, my bride, drip honey; Honey and milk are under your tongue.

Most of the Bible commentators I checked think honey and milk in this verse refer to the richness of the land of Canaan. No, it doesn't! Honey and milk as used here have nothing to do with the land of Canaan! No doubt these commentators don't know how to kiss, either. Real kissing tastes good! That's what the verse is saying. Solomon connects honey and milk to his bride's tongue, not Canaan. If this isn't a reference to French kissing, I don't know what is.

When was the last time you were decently kissed by your spouse? I'll bet it's been a while. You two know how to kiss each other. You used to do it all the time. It's time to get back to that kind of kissing. You can start right away. (*Men Are Clams*, pp.232-234)

Watch Romantic Movies

Just the two of you sit down and watch a romantic movie. You can get out the old classics like *Casablanca, To Have and Have Not, Holiday Inn,* or go with some more current titles like *Sleepless in Seattle*, the new *Pride and Prejudice*, the remake of *Shakespeare in Love,* and oh yeah, the Tarzan and Jane movies.

Then follow the advice from David Clarke in his book,

Sit together on the love seat or couch. Not one of you in a chair and one on the couch. Not both in chairs. Come on! Being four or five feet apart defeats the whole purpose! You are close so you can touch. Kiss. Make out. As you watch the movie, the romantic interplay on the screen transfers to the two of you and your relationship. It's not Humphrey Bogart falling in love with Lauren Bacall. It's Bob falling in love with Betty! (*Men Are Clams*, pp.208-209).

Slow Dancing

Put some romantic music on the stereo or CD player. You could play beautiful, soft instrumental pieces or some of your favorite love songs.

Music is powerful. It can touch us and move us. We use music to worship, to open up our hearts to God. We can use music to create romance, to open up our hearts to each other.

With the lights down low, just hold each other close and slowly sway to the music. You don't need dancing lessons. If you're going to dance in public, get lessons. But in the privacy of your own home, no one's watching. If you're having trouble talking on a deeper level, try slow dancing before talking. It's amazing how it can open you up! (*Men Are Clams,* p. 208)

We'd like to go further with the dancing concept and suggest strip dancing. This is often the natural consequences of slow dancing. Hey, it's in the privacy of your own home. Slowly make your way to the bedroom away from any possibility of the children seeing you and begin to undress one another as you dance. Ladies, every once in a while, you may even allow your husband to take the more direct approach and forget the clothes and slow dance in the nude.

Candlelight Dinner

Here are some pointers to create a special night. Put the kids to bed early. Use the good china (paper plates and cups just don't set the mood) and a nice tablecloth. Put on instrumental background music. Order a couple of great dishes from a good restaurant. (*Men Are Clams,* p. 208)

Pull her chair out for her and sit close together. Pour a glass of her favorite drink. Lock arms and feed each other during the meal or during dessert. You know you are really successful if you can't finish the meal. Hubba, hubba! Be sure to dress up (before you dress down). Scented candles are really romantic for the bedroom, so don't forget the candles and matches!

The Scenic Drive Date

When you do not have the time or the money to get away on a trip, even for a weekend, a scenic drive can give you a break and relaxation that you may need as a couple or family. Drive along the ocean, into the mountains, out of the city and into the country. During the holidays, cities put on great light displays, so you may want to drive from the country or suburb into the city during that time. Or during the spring or fall when the trees are changing and/or flowers are blooming, take a relaxing drive with the windows down and your favorite music on.

It is a great time to talk about your relationship. Enjoy the scenery, comment on its beauty and how it makes you feel. Hold hands and walk together. We are fortunate that we live near the beach so the sunsets are amazing and the beach a beautiful place to take a walk. Before you turn around and head back to the house, stop and get an ice cream and quietly enjoy the experience. Sometimes we cannot wait for the long vacation or even the weekend, and it is those short breaks that make the difference and provide unforgettable memories.

Date Night
Shared by Van and Charlotte, married 30 years

We own our own real estate company and both of us work there. You would think that we would have a lot of time together but it is not so. Most of our inter-action time is about business during the day, and most of our nights are filled with appointments with our clients, both buyers and sellers. It would be easy to grow apart and become strangers living in the same home and working at the same business.

To keep our marriage alive, we maintain a Friday

night date night—our time to blow off steam from a hectic week, be personal with one another, and enjoy each other.

———•———

A Calendar
Shared by Randy and Peggy, married 26 years

One Christmas I opened a gift from my husband, Randy, and it was a calendar for the next year. It looked nice enough, but it was just a calendar so I quickly tossed it aside to begin opening more exciting looking gifts with the frilly wrapping.

After I finished opening my gifts, I began shuffling one by one back through them again. I really enjoy savoring every Christmas moment. As I picked up the calendar, Randy, with a huge grin on his face, prodded me to take a look inside. I flipped through the pages wondering, "What are all these markings for?" When I took a closer look, I realized that these weren't just markings, they were specifically planned "date nights" for the two of us. I couldn't believe what I was seeing. My heart was touched by what my husband had done. He had lovingly and thoughtfully planned special "date nights" months in advance, just for us! Clutching my calendar to my chest, I hugged Randy and thanked him for his wonderful gift. Amazingly, what I had moments earlier tossed aside as just a "so-so" gift became my favorite gift of all.

Truly, my heart was deeply moved that Christmas by Randy's thoughtfulness. Our lives and schedules get so busy, so I felt especially loved by the fact that he had carefully set aside time just to spend with me. Of all my Christmas gifts and memories, this is one of my all-time favorites!

Many years ago, Randy began a tradition in our house that still continues to this day. Twelve days before Christmas, he will conspicuously hide a simple gift and attach a romantic poem with it. Each following day, I find a gift and a poem hidden somewhere.

These gifts are not elaborate at all. In fact, they may be as simple as a piece of candy, but the notes that come with them are what touch my heart the most. I love to read words that Randy has penned just for me. And each day is so completely different. They may be funny, serious, or frivolous, but they always have a romantic twist. And each day during those twelve days of Christmas, I eagerly anticipate reading the next one. The longer we are married, the more I realize that in our relationship it is those simple things that really do mean a lot.

Dates do not have to cost much of anything at all. We love to go to the beach in the evening and walk hand in hand and watch the sunset. Packing up dinner and taking it to the park is always nice, and afterwards you can share your leftovers with the ducks and squirrels.

Sometimes we have dinner at home and go out for a late night run to the ice cream shop to share a large, hot fudge sundae. We love going to the mall just to walk hand and hand and window shop. (Notice I said, "window shop." Many men do not like shopping, and my man is one of them, but he does seem to enjoy walking through the mall with me.)

The new bookstores are great for date nights.

Sometimes we spend an hour or so perusing the racks of our favorite store to see what is new on the market. We get a kick out of showing each other what we have found. We realize more and more how important it is to take time to be alone together. It is always nice to do the "evening out at a restaurant and a movie," but we have learned through the years that some of the nicest dates we have ever experienced did not cost much of anything at all!

Anniversaries

It is good to remember your anniversary with a card, candy, or dinner out. Remembering your anniversary says that the date is special to you. If you have a hard time remembering, jot it on your calendar. Take time in planning to make the day special! You do not have to spend lots of money to make it so. Blocking off time for each other is a good gift, and it does not cost a cent. You can also make an anniversary special with a short getaway to celebrate, enjoy each other, and reflect on your relationship.

Have a Holy Day
Shared by Nick and Kathy, married 32 years

After laboring faithfully for many years in the pastorate, I noticed that like most marriages, mine was suffering from marriage's most common disease: LCA (Lack of Consistent Attention). Like most dedicated men, I always waited until I had enough time or money to fix the problem with a big, two-week vacation. But by the time that happened, the damage was already done. I did not realize that most marital stress does not require "fixing" but rather, "overcoming." Fixing takes money and time and never lasts, but overcoming requires a little regular consistent attention. For years my wife had asked me for a regular time when she could count on having my undivided attention. And since needs pop up on a daily and weekly basis, I needed to be exclusively available to her with that kind of frequency.

So we decided to make a weekly "holy day," with all its rights and privileges. For us, that day would be Monday. From sunrise Monday to sunrise Tuesday I became invisible and non-existent to the world and particularly to the ministry. With the exception of a severe accident or death, I would not respond to anyone but Kathy. I do not answer the phone and am never available for any kind of talk, meeting, or event.

We do all our own home remodeling and yard work, so Mondays I strap on my tool belt and attack Kathy's ever expanding HGTV-inspired list of house improvements and repairs. This I do with love for my wife and a lot of cheer, particularly since she is always working right alongside me. We usually plan ahead and try to purchase materials in advance so our time can be most fruitful. Later in the day we clean up and often go out for dinner or just relax together in the TV room.

As a result of our holy day, my wife knows that "we" are a priority. The door to our marital peace stays closed to the Accuser, and our working relationship is strengthened. Additionally, we made a commitment many years ago to have daily prayer and fellowship in the Word together. As we come up on our 31st anniversary, we can say with authority that marriages that suffer from LCA can be turned around by couples making commitments to give each other regular consistent attention that are holy and unbreakable. Marriages are not "fixed"; they overcome. And overcoming takes a holy partnership.

———•———

Notes to Go

Kathy always leaves creative encouraging notes in various compartments of my luggage or clothing when I am traveling—cards of appreciation, written prayers asking for God's best, or coupons promising a romantic intimate night when I return. For instance, on a recent trip I found two coupons—one was a promise of a body massage and the other a night out. The good problem I have is to decide whether to use them both on the same night or on separate nights. No matter how many times she gives me notes, it always brings a smile to my face.

As I write this, it dawns on me that I could do the same for her in return, something I will personally apply on my next trip. Her small expressions of love remind me of the great relationship we have and serves as a preemptive strike against the sexual temptations that so many men face as they travel. Regardless of how fruitful and inspiring are my trips, I can't wait to get home and enjoy Kathy's loving embrace. As a general rule, I always try to bring home a small gift of some kind for Kathy and each of the kids. It is usually very inexpensive, but it lets them know they are always in my thoughts.

Keeping the fire burning in your relationship will help your marriage when you have the pressures of kids, finances, and daily doldrums. It will help to solidify your relationship so you can continue to keep your marriage strong in the face of daily confrontations.

CHAPTER 7

GODLY COUNSEL

A divorced mother with two children read this manu-
script and remarked, "If I could have had the counsel that is
in this book, I might still be married." Thankfully we don't
have to let experience be our only teacher because learning
by our mistakes is so painful. Learning from others and
from God's Word is God's loving way of helping us to avoid
emotional and mental pain.

Godly counsel comes from godly people who have
walked out God's Word. They have grown to be "trees of
righteousness, planted by the Lord." Isaiah 61:3 In this
chapter we encourage you to pick from the fruit of others to
benefit your marriage.

Our first counsel is for the newly married. One problem
that newlyweds experience is the proper boundaries of their
parents concerning their relationship, home, and children.
Someone who has lived under their parent's authority for
20+ years and then gets married needs to build a new relationship and put boundaries on their parents.

In Genesis, God said regarding marriage that a man will
leave his father and mother and cleave to his wife. This is
why we have a father giving away the bride. It is not merely

Godly Counsel

ceremonial but rather intensely spiritual because it represents the transfer of responsibility and authority to a new home and marriage being established. Walking that out in a relationship is essential.

The couple that allows well-meaning in-laws to influence their relationship in an unhealthy way is destined for trouble. Yet at the same time there is a need to use those in-laws as a source of guidance and strength at the request of the couple. Building boundaries and at the same time conveying love and respect is important. Grandpa and Grandma can be a huge blessing to the children (and a break for Mom and Dad especially during the younger years).

The preparation for leaving and cleaving should take place during the engagement and pre-marital counseling stage. During this time it is good to begin to establish how you will handle your finances and where you will attend church. Both your parents will have had an influence in those decisions by having raised you, but now a new home and a new way of doing things will be established. The leaving and cleaving process will continue as you grow together in the relationship.

Jane had to make a choice to go back to the city or follow her husband, Tarzan, into the jungle. Jane said, "My place is with my husband." Sometimes we will have to make a choice for the good of our marital relationship over other relationships as we see in the testimony by Tony and Kari.

Leave and Cleave
Shared by Tony and Kari, married 7 years

I believe that when God said, "A man shall leave his father and mother and cleave to his wife," He had me in mind. I have learned that principle in a very practical sense. I did not have a problem leaving and cleaving, but my mother and some of my relatives did. It is hard to leave and cleave when your family is still clinging to you.

Though we love and pray for our extended families, we had to set some healthy boundaries. My mother had a difficult time letting go. She and other family members were dragging their dysfunction into our new life together. It went beyond meddling in our affairs to speaking maligning words toward my wife. My mother, who is a widow, saw herself as losing a son rather than gaining a daughter-in-law. She was threatened by my love for Kari. This caused her to openly cut my wife down. When I sought to correct her, she threatened to cut herself off from me entirely. It got to the point where we put a "call block" on our phone.

Cleaving to my wife meant I would not entertain these accusations. I always backed Kari up. It also meant not tolerating any malicious speech directed toward Kari by a family member. I learned to put a stop to it before it ever got going. When the idle threats of losing my mother's love were made, I let her know I loved and honored her as my mother, but my loyalties were now with Kari.

My family has been able to respect these boundaries for the most part. However, when the boundaries are still tried from time to time, we are quick to enforce them. Protecting our marriage in this manner has truly drawn Kari and me together. We have developed a deep loyalty and trust for one another. We are careful not to accuse or blame each other as well. This has also helped us with our business. When we married, I made Kari a full partner in my already established business. Occasionally family members don't like her decisions and try to bypass her. They soon find out that her decisions are mine as well. We are so grateful we took a stand for one another against my family's inappropriate behavior and involvement. It saved us from wounds through words and mistrust that could have destroyed our marriage. By practically implementing what it means to "leave and cleave," what was a threat to our marriage became an instrument that strengthened our relationship instead.

Accepting Each Other's Family
Shared by Ralph and Myla, married 15 years

One thing that has sustained our marriage is our acceptance of each other's families. Ralph was so supporting of my mother's needs and my time commitments to her when she was suffering with emphysema. I had to be with her for hours at her home, then later in the hospital and rehabilitation centers. Eventually she lived with us. The last 18 months of her life, both of us and our son, Nathan, who was six at the time, took shifts giving mom needed breathing treatments every four hours around the clock. The three of us assisted her with her tracheotomy as well. During all of this, Ralph never once complained or got angry, even though we all were under stress. That made me appreciate him even more than ever before.

My (Ralph's) side of the family tested Myla as well. My grandmother had Alzheimer's disease. Myla picked her up faithfully every Sunday morning and would take her to church. This went on for several years, even when I had to work. She also accepted my younger brother who had drug and alcohol addictions. He had many schemes and ideas and was downright unlovable at times. She was so concerned for him; he was on the top of her prayer list for years.

Break the Soul Ties

There are good traits we inherited from our parents, and there are some not-so-good ones we acquired. Often these not-so-good ones are brought into our home life. To prevent making some of the same mistakes our parents made, first, forgive your parents for those areas you realize that were negative but are now a part of your life. Even if they are not alive, as my dad was not, forgive and release them.

Second, accept responsibility for your behavior. One way I do that is to confess that I learned some wrong behaviors while growing up, but now I make a choice to be different. It is more than "My dad was an alcoholic and now I have a problem with addictions." At one point I saw that my dad had a lack of respect for my mom and women, and it was affecting my marriage. It was not until we had children that my father's temper become evident in me. I had to forgive my dad, recognize it, and at the same time declare that it as not a part of my life. I had to replace that temper by building a character filled with love, patience, and temperance.

Breaking a soul tie means declaring that there are some attitudes and actions that I acquired through my parents and that I will maintain the good but break off the bad. I choose not to adopt that way of living but desire to create a new way, a new pattern for me and my family.

If you are like me and did not have a correct role model to look to in your father or mother, there are others who are willing to be mentors.

Make Sure the Closets are Clean

Many have entered marriage carrying wounds from previous relationships. Current problems may occur because of them. If your mate is over-sensitive, over-reacting, or insecure, it may be due to an old relationship. It also may be due to certain incorrect behaviors that have been learned. For example, the way a wife reacts to her husband may be more of a learned response than a response to the actual situation. If communication about the problem is difficult, you need to find counseling to help heal the past and create a healthier present.

Be Flexible

Life happens, people change, and our circumstances change. Remain flexible and allow things to develop. I can give many examples of how our course totally changed from what we anticipated. We thought we would minister to a middle-sized traditional church. God walked us through a small church, street ministry, mission field, and city-wide ministry. God was faithful to prepare us for each new endeavor but we had to be flexible with our plans.

Accidents, deaths, loss of job and other circumstances can cause stress in any relationship. Remaining faithful in your relationship with God and knowing He is in control of all situations can help to give a perspective to handle each challenge.

Counseling, Counseling, Counseling

Our counsel to those not yet married is to seek premarital counseling. Premarital counseling saved me from marrying the wrong person and confirmed who was the right one for me. A good counselor can give an objective point of view. If he/she believes marriage is good for you at that time, then he/she will give you possible problem areas to guard against. Get counseling before the mole hill becomes a mountain.

Often it's us men who are reluctant to get counseling because we think we can work out our own problems. Sometimes there are problems that are not going to go away by themselves, and you might need the special attention of a third party's help and insight. Counseling can be costly, although some insurance cover certain counselors. If you live in Florida, the state government gives couples who will take pre-marital counseling $32 off their marriage license. Local pastors are usually willing to give counsel (they are free or very cheap). Larger churches have a counseling department. For those who have been married awhile, be willing to get counseling about your differences or any other problems especially if you have not had a benefit of premarital counseling. Your pride is not as important as saving your marriage and family. Save your marriage from avoidable grief and difficulty by humbling yourself and getting help.

Counseling is not only important before entering marriage, but after the wedding and ongoing through the marriage. The next three couples give their experience and establish the need for counseling.

Christian Counseling
Shared by Rusty and Gay, married 25 years

When difficulties occur, and they will, it may be

necessary to receive sound biblical counseling. View Christian counselors as ones who can come alongside and be a mentor to you and your spouse. They can guide you through difficult times and help you recognize blind spots in your relationship. We found that the multitude of our responsibilities and a misappropriation of priorities in our lives took a toll on our marriage. The counselor helped us begin to see through each other's eyes and recognize the needs of one another. We also came to understand with a greater clarity how much Jesus loved us and gave us a perfect example to love each other.

Ongoing Tune-ups

Shared by Dale and Kaye, married 40 years

Kay was 18 and I was 20 when we married. Kay worked as a secretary for an insurance agency, and I held down a job and pastored a church. Several years into our marriage, we were still hard at work, but our marriage was failing.

A lot of changes happen between 20 and 30 years of age. We were changing and growing but not together. We finally reached a point of desperation and had a meeting of the minds. We came away from it with a joint decision. We concluded that if we worked as hard at our marriage as we do at our jobs, we could have a great one.

We realized that many more changes were ahead. We were going to change physically, spiritually, and psychologically. Those changes would be subtle, coming every few months or at least years. We had to explore together where we were at and where we thought the changes were leading us. We began regularly evaluating what our marriage needed and what areas we should work on. Part of our commitment to work on our marriage was done through marriage seminars and counselors. They both give us "tune-ups." We have regular physical exams, and saw that we need to do the same with our marriage. Even after 40 years of marriage, we go for periodic counseling. It helps to keep us problem free rather than focused on problem solving. It's great to have a safe place to vent frustration.

As a pastor, I initially felt that all I needed was the Word of God and not any seminar or counseling. However, the Bible also tells us, "Through the counsel of many there is success." We went into our first counseling session very reluctantly. It didn't take long to see many blind spots brought to light and our need to have an objective person speak into our marriage and help us find the areas we needed to work on. I recommend spending the money to get counseling regularly even if everything is OK. Usually you can find counselors who will give you a break if the cost is prohibitive. Divorce will cost quite a bit more.

One good marriage seminar is Rekindling the Romance, put on by Dennis Rainey and Family Ministries. It's a one-day seminar that can help rekindle your love for one another and encourage further counseling to keep the flame burning. Another is Marriage Encounter—you can find more about these by going to www.marriageencounter.com. Another seminar is Laugh Your Way to a Better Marriage by Mark Gungor. See www.laughyourway.com.

Take a Personality Profile Test

The Disc Personality profile test given by Moody Bible Institute is particularly effective. It shares how to interact with different personalities. It relates to characters in the Bible and their personalities and demonstrates how God dealt with them according to their makeup. Another personality profile which also adds a spiritual gift test is "Uniquely You" by Dr. Mels Carbonell.

Every engaged couple needs to do this before marriage. If you haven't taken this test as a married couple, I encourage you to do so. I wish I would have taken it much earlier in our marriage. It has helped me to understand myself and the affect my personality has on others and how to relate better to my wife and others. Now having studied these personalities, we can see the various traits in each of our children and do a better job in raising them.

Birds of a Feather Flock Together

Abandoned as a small child, Tarzan had to adapt to his surroundings not only to survive but also to succeed in his jungle life. Because he did so, he was labelled the King of the Jungle.

Our surroundings or the people we associate with can have a significant impact on our lives. Unfortunately many of us tend to simply adapt to the negative elements and not seek out positive ones. It would serve us well to surround ourselves with people who want to be successful in their marriages.

If you want to be a better businessman, for example, you will hang out with people who want to do the same. If you want a lasting, healthy family, then it would do you well to socialize with those who are achieving or at least serious about the same domestic goals and values. It does not mean you alienate yourself from others, but if you associate with those who often complain about their spouse or cheat on them, it can become a bad influence. Guard your marriage by guarding your heart and mind in what it receives from others.

Finding a Mentor
Shared by Andy and Jill, married 23 years

Being around other couples who want the same things as we do in our marriage has been a great benefit. Those relationships have led us into deeper accountability with a few couples. We give them permission to speak into our lives individually and as a couple, and they do the same.

It is not done throughout a formal setting where we go through a check list, but it happens naturally as we take in a movie or go out for dinner together. There are situations that we do not discuss in a group. Often the guys will go golfing or the gals go shopping in order to share more freely. Through casual conversation we will ask, "Have you thought about this or tried that?" Through understanding what we are or are not doing, we are equally stirred to improve ourselves and our marriages.

Some of the relationships have been a great encouragement to Andy. After retiring from major league baseball, Andy pursued a second career. He had a great relationship with my father, but he passed away a year after Andy's retirement. Andy missed having that friendship with on older man who was a father figure to him. My dad had a wonderful boss, and so there was an immediate trust factor since he was a respected Christian businessman and a beloved friend of my dad. Andy approached him about giving guidance as a businessman, father, and husband. Even though Andy was in his mid-thirties he realized much more of his life as a man, father, and husband was yet to be lived. Having such a mentor has been an enormous encouragement and safety net for both of us.

Celebrate Your Differences

Let's face it—we are different. But instead of being negative about our differences, celebrate them. Life would be boring if we all were alike. Check out this list of why it is great to be a guy (and girls, why we men are thankful you are not!).

Great Reasons to be a Guy
- Phone conversations are over in 30 seconds flat.
- A five-day vacation requires only one suitcase.
- You can go to the bathroom without a support group.
- You can leave the motel bed unmade.
- You can kill your own food.
- You get extra credit for the slightest act of thoughtfulness.
- Wedding plans take care of themselves.
- Your underwear is $10 for a three-pack.
- Everything on your face stays its original color.
- Three pairs of shoes are more than enough.
- You don't have to clean your apartment if the meter reader is coming.
- Car mechanics tell you the truth.
- You can quietly watch a game with your buddy for hours without ever thinking, "He must be mad at me."

- Gray hair and wrinkles only add character.
- You can drop by to see a friend without having to bring a little gift.
- If another guy shows up at the same party in the same outfit, you just become lifelong friends.
- Your pals can be trusted never to trap you with, "So, notice anything different?"
- You are not expected to know the names of more than five colors.
- You are unable to see wrinkles in your clothes.
- The same hairstyle lasts for years, maybe decades.
- Your belly usually hides your big hips.
- One wallet and one pair of shoes, one color, all seasons.
- You can "do" your nails with a pocketknife.
- Christmas shopping can be accomplished for 25 relatives, on December 24th in 45 minutes.

Girls, the list above shows that you can appreciate your man even if you become annoyed with his idiosyncrasies as well. Isn't that what makes our lives fun, interesting, and challenging? We don't understand how we can be attracted to or miss some of this behavior, but we know we would. Men and women are different, and we should celebrate these differences instead of being negative about them.

Togetherness is great, but allowing your mate to have other pursuits or interests also helps them to grow as an individual. This brings them greater fulfillment and you can better enjoy the person you married. They will love you more for creating those avenues. These interests can be positive to your relationship, but be careful that these interests are not too time consuming and take you away from family.

CHAPTER 8

MONEY, MATING, AND OTHER MATTERS

Did you ever stop to think why Tarzan and Jane were so happy even though they lived in a tree house? The answer is easy—they were out of debt and had no worries. Yes, this might be an exaggeration, but it does emphasize the point that an unwise decision, like getting into debt, is bondage and can steal joy out of your marriage.

This is our M & M chapter. Like the candy, it will give you small doses of advice to make your relationship sweeter. The proverb tells us, "The counsel of many (in this case many friends) brings success" (Proverbs 11:14;15:22). Pay close attention to the two areas covered in this chapter on finances and sex. Abuse and neglect in these areas have caused many marriages to end.

MONEY

Budget together. Many problems arise with the way the money is spent. We have agreed that if it's *our money*, then we need to develop *our budget*. When unexpected expenses come up that are beyond the budget, then we communicate about the expense and how it might be paid. In setting a budget, it helps both parties to understand the real expenses of running a household, buying clothes, groceries, and all the other necessary things. It's good for the husband to do the shopping with the wife at least once in a while to get an idea of what things cost. (Setting a budget helps also to jointly pick out affordable insurance.)

By budgeting together you can agree on what to buy, when you can buy it, and how much you can spend. This takes a lot of stress out of your relationship. It allows you to focus on marriage and family and not material things. This is particularly important during the holidays when emotions run high. (Unfortunately so do the interest charges that come with your January credit card bill.)

Living Trust

Making a living trust or will is important. Planning what happens when one partner dies also increases your bonding. You can't make a will or living trust or buy cemetery plots unless you are serious about fulfilling the "until death do us part " words of your wedding vows. This sends a message to the whole family of permanence because you are in effect saying, "We plan to be faithful to the end." I encourage people to get a living trust. It can be easily changed and helps to prevent probate.

Staying Out of Debt

I remember the time we were looking for dining room chairs. A friend had made us a beautiful table, and we needed chairs to go with it. I looked and looked but every-thing was so expensive, and we couldn't afford the hefty price. So I waited and prayed for chairs. Several months later I saw a sale in the paper for unfinished chairs. I raced down to check them out and was able to buy four for the price I would have normally paid for two chairs.

We have had a philosophy since the beginning of our marriage to remain debt free. Other than the major expense of a house payment, we have kept to that philosophy. By living within your means, it takes stress and pressures out of the marriage. It also frees you up as individuals and a family to do things together and have a life without the burden of feeling like you have to always work to pay all the bills.

This can be hard at times because our human flesh cries out constantly for the finer things of life. We want to take advantage of the "no interest for several years" or the other deals that come along. It gives us the temporary high of getting what we want, but it has a ball and chain with it

Patience and self-control go a long way toward staying out of debt. You need to be patient to wait for the right deals to come along or until you save enough to afford it. Live within your means and stay out of debt as much as possible. Two spouses having to work because of lack of self-control in credit buying eventually sacrifices the family. The stress of such financial burdens can tear apart a home. If you're in debt, work with someone to get out and stay out! Be content with what you have.

It's Our Money
Shared by Ralph and Myla, married 15 years

We have an agreement that I (Ralph) would make all the major decisions, and Myla would make all the minor decisions. So far there haven't been any major decisions (just kidding). There was a time when we did have to make a major decision concerning how we would deal with money. We married late and were both accustomed to having our own money and several checking accounts. One day I came across a woman in need that both Myla and I knew. Her car needed repair and it would cost $700 that she didn't have. I had the money and gave it to her. Later as I shared with Myla, she was upset that I had not confided in her before making such a major financial decision even though she would have agreed to it. This incident made us stop and look at how we were operating our finances.

We came to several decisions that have helped us in our marriage. The first one was to consult one another before any major purchase. The second one was that we would both know what money is coming in and agree on what goes out. In order to do that, we decided that we needed to be one literally in our checking account. We did not want to say, "This is my money and that is yours." It is ours and it is God's money. I, Ralph, was better at keeping the checkbook so that became my job. These roles have eliminated stress and blame casting and have caused us to pull together during lean times. When God said the two shall become one, we believe that it includes money. It has enhanced the very commitment we have made to be one in mind, body, and spirit.

MATING

Men, listen, good sex just doesn't happen. It is going to take time to prep your wife. She might want to talk first, and you will need to listen to her. Your wife might need a back rub or foot rub to get her interested and ready for you. Here is a good adage that lines up with our book title, "If you want her to swing on your vine, give her the time."

When it comes to sex, let's face it, it can be an uncharted territory because of demands on you as individuals.

By the end of the day, especially on the woman's part, you can be physically, emotionally and mentally drained by the day's activities. Hubby can be pumped to enjoy sex and the wife just wants to be left alone. We have found that preparation for that event can help in furthering the experience.

Husbands, if you want that sexual experience you desire, do some things to let your wife know it, and she will be anticipating it instead of not wanting sex. For example, you might give her a call during the day and let her know how special she is and how much you want to be with her that night. You can make some remarks that will slowly light the flame for later. This is only the beginning of preparation and will get you into the bedroom (or any other creative place). There are also other ways to create the mood such as lighting candles, putting petals on the bed, or playing soft music. Be creative and you will get good results.

Once you prepare in these ways, you can't stop there. A sexual encounter is more than the act itself. Take the time to enjoy each other—talk, kiss, laugh, touch...You will be pleased by your results from making preparations. Being married gives us an ability to be creative, fun, and fulfilled in our sexual intimacy. Sexual intimacy should be an extension or expression of our intellectual, emotional, and spiritual intimacy. Finding ways to please one another sexually is good. Usually real communication helps as well. If you are engaged to be married, a good book as a means of sexual preparation is *The Act of Marriage* by Tim LaHaye.

Kinky Is Not Cool

When we go beyond the creative and natural ways to enjoy one another, we are treading on dangerous ground. We are, in fact, inviting a spirit of perversion and lust into our marriage. Lust has an insatiable appetite. If you get into adult sex toys or bondage, for instance, you are degrading your mate by making them a sex object and not a cherished and respected husband or wife. Some couples think it is OK to watch pornographic films together to arouse themselves because they are doing it together. If being together is not enough, real love is missing. The couple that continues in any of these practices will eventually find themselves discontented with one another and be tempted to try new partners to satisfy their sex appetite. Sex is addictive and seductive. As a couple, we cannot underestimate its power when it goes beyond its proper boundaries in marriage.

After viewing either nudes from *Playboy, Playgirl* and *Penthouse,* or slides of abstract art, undergraduate men and women at Arizona State University were asked to evaluate their mates. At the American Psychological Association Convention, researches reported that the erotica had at least some short-term effects. Those exposed to it rated their mates less attractive sexually and said they felt less love for them.

Stop and think. Most of those pictures are fabricated taking out any defects. If those pictured people were available they certainly would not be available to the likes of most of us. By viewing pornographic material, it can only create fantasies in our mind that can do nothing to satisfy the true love we need. We lose appreciation for the person who can give us that love.

If you find yourself enslaved to wrong sexual practices even inside your marriage, break it off now. Turn away from them and ask God to cleanse you. Return to purity and respect your marriage mate. Don't underestimate the power of sex—a little porn, a little flirting, a little straying. Give no room for any of it. You'll only get burnt!

For this reason the Proverb tells us, "Let your fountain

be blessed, and rejoice in the wife of your youth...let her breasts satisfy you at all times, be exhilarated always with her love." By keeping our focus on our mates, we won't become distracted and dissatisfied.

Ladies, be Jane and come out one night in a sexy piece made of fake fur. Just kidding! But you can arouse your husband's interest with an appealing nightie that is sexy and in good taste. Tell him he's Tarzan, King of the Jungle (or at least the bedroom). Be creative and do something that builds him up. You want him beating on his chest giving his jungle cry, "AAAAAH, AAAH." Then, you will have him focused on you, and your imagination can fill in the rest.

False Expectations

Understand the difference between love and romance. George Bernard Shaw wrote, "When two people are under the influence of the most violent, most insane, most delusive and most transient of passions, they are required to swear that they will remain in that excited, abnormal and exhausting condition continuously until death to us part." Like many of us, Mr. Shaw is confusing true deep love with romance or erotic passion that is portrayed on Hollywood movies and soap operas.

New Webster's Dictionary defines romance as "a fictitious tale of wonderful, extraordinary events characterized by much imagination and idealization; without basis in fact; an exaggeration or falsehood." Every relationship needs romance, but no relationship can live there. Expecting a marriage to sustain that level is as far fetched as Bernard Shaw writes. It's a false expectation that can only lead to disappointment and steal your opportunity to experience true love and intimacy. True love is not one big roll in the hay or one big swing in the jungle, but it is the daily kiss on the lips before you go off to work. It's the little things that keep the flames of love burning deep. Just like a good fire that has burned itself to red hot coals, with additional wood, a small breeze will turn the coals into a blazing fire. A good marriage that burns deep with consistent love just needs the slightest look, the smallest act of passion, or a tiny gift of appreciation to turn on the flames of romantic love.

Maturity is the ability to hold onto the ideal but live in the present day's reality. This brings a balance between knowing there is always room for improvement and appreciating the improvements that have been made in your marriage and family life. In high school I rarely cared about my appearance until I met Mary Sue. No one had to tell me to dress nice, comb my hair, or make sure I put on deodorant then. I had a crush on Mary Sue and I wanted to impress her.

Possibly you have had a similar experience. When you were falling in love, no one had to tell you to be considerate, dress nice, or do spontaneous loving acts. Unfortunately, somewhere over the years of a relationship, we begin to take each other for granted.

There is a verse in the book of Revelation where Jesus tells a church that they have lost their first love. The solution to this lost love was to repent and do the first works again. The same solution can be used for those who have lost their first love for one another in a marriage. Do the first works again. Do the things you used to do when you were falling in love with your spouse the first time.

Going for God's Perfect Will
Shared by Tommy and Julie, married 23 years

Tommy was a rodeo cowboy. The lifestyle that

goes with the rodeo is not what I would call family friendly. There is a great deal about the rodeo that makes a wife uneasy. After nine years of marriage, my fears and suspicions became a reality. Tommy confessed that he had several extramarital affairs. The last one was four years prior to his telling me. He had grown spiritually and was convinced he needed to come clean. Of course, I was devastated. I had saved myself until marriage for the man I love. I hurt so much I wanted to die. I could not forgive him or forget the many acts of unfaithfulness and betrayal. When he would pass me in the house I would hit him. We would be sleeping in bed, and I'd jump on him and begin to fight without being provoked. Bringing it up and throwing it in his face was a favorite form of revenge. I wanted him to hurt like I hurt. Repeatedly I said, "I ought to leave you." The kids wondered what had gotten into me to be so mean to their father. We did not tell them what had happened, so I looked like the bad guy. I finally came to a place where I had to decide to leave or stay.

A friend told me, "You have every right to leave, but do you want to be in God's permissible will or God's perfect will?" "It's not fair," I said. "Why do I have to be the one to decide? I didn't have the affairs."

Shortly thereafter I decided I wanted God's perfect will. The bottom line is I still loved Tommy deeply, and I knew by the abuse he absorbed from me that he loved me too.

I forgave Tommy from my heart. Now, the problem was how to forget. The thoughts and pictures in my mind of his unfaithfulness haunted me, yet I knew I had forgiven him. The bitterness would creep in each time I gave way to the thoughts. I began practicing supplanting those thoughts with what the Bible calls "putting my mind on things above." I intentionally thought about things that were noble and praiseworthy—good things about my husband, marriage, and our life and family. Little by little the wrong thoughts became less frequent and have almost disappeared entirely. Tommy's earning back my trust by remaining faithful.

Together we minister to the rodeo cowboys and their families. Being committed to helping the brokenness in others has helped us heal and grow. God has used my willingness to forgive and forget and turned our broken marriage into His plan for our lives.

Go with the Flow
Shared by Gloria and Dave, married 30 years

Our marriage has thrived for 30 years because early on we learned to pick our battles. By this I mean we don't waste our time and energy arguing over little things, such as his not zipping his pants when he puts them in the laundry or my not being ready to leave a gathering when he is ready to leave. We try to put the other person's feelings and happiness first. We also discuss those things that irritate us so the other person is aware of them as well. When we consider the other's happiness, it takes the selfish emphasis off those dumb things that could upset us and our marriage. Instead, it helps us focus on our love for each other and encourages us to be kind to one another. It is more important for us to be together than to get our own way, so we have learned to go with the flow.

How to Gain Respect
Shared by Bob and Gail, married 31 years

After working to help Bob through medical school, we began to have our family. At that time, we decided I would stay home to raise the children. Though I have no regrets about staying home, this did produce some problems. We were both carrying emotional and mental baggage from our childhood. My fear of abandonment brought about an unhealthy dependence because Bob had an anger and control problem. Also my Christian walk caused problems since Bob was not saved.

Bob, meanwhile, was becoming very successful as an orthopedic surgeon. The money and power that came with success eroded what little respect he had for me as his wife and a stay-at-home mom. His disrespect turned into explosive anger, and he became verbally abusive. Yet, our home had many happy times which caused me to remain in denial that things were deteriorating. My understanding was that I was to tolerate whatever he dished out because I was a submissive wife. I knew I wasn't supposed to be a doormat, but I felt like an emotional doormat. I felt unsupported in crises, verbally disrespected, and the scapegoat for anything that went wrong.

Were it not for fear of abandonment, I would have insisted on counseling long before our problems intensified. When I came out of denial and recognized the extent of the problems, I misunderstood how to draw proper boundaries. In my frustration, I thought yelling back was a way of standing up for myself.

We finally went to a counselor that Bob approved of. I finally began to learn how to draw boundaries when I was being verbally abused. I became willing to confront him, and he began to find respect for me. I formulated a list of past hurts that I needed to forgive him for. He acknowledged how he had hurt me and asked for my forgiveness. I told Bob I still loved him deeply. This inner strength Bob saw in me gained his respect not only for myself but for my Lord, Jesus Christ. Not long thereafter, Bob gave his life to Christ. With Christ in our lives and mutual respect toward one another, we now experience the joy of intimacy.

OTHER MATTERS THAT MATTER
The grass isn't always greener

Joyce Landorf tells in her book, *Tough and Tender* of a man she calls George, who used to work at her husband's bank.

George had a recent divorce which led him into the swinging scene of sexual liberation. He was one of the most envied bachelors around: he had a beach apartment, beauty queens in and out nightly with no hassles. He had it made. One afternoon George came up to my husband's desk and haltingly said, "Dick, could I talk with you for a moment?" George con-

tinued, "You know Dick, I really got it made. I'm free
from the attachments of marriage. I've got this great
place on the beach, and I go to bed with one sexy girl
after another. I come and go as I please, and I do my
own thing. But something is really bothering me and
I can't figure it out. Every morning as I get dressed
for work I look into the mirror and I think, 'What
was last night's sexy little game all about?' Sure the
girl was good looking and she left this morning
without bugging me, but is that all there is in life? If
this lifestyle is what every guy thinks he wants, why
am I so depressed? Why do I feel a cold nothing-
ness?"

He stooped and leaned closer to Dick and quietly
continued, "I know the guys here think it would be
fantastic to have this kind of liberated freedom but
honestly, Dick, I hate this life. You know what I'd really like? I'd like to go home tonight, smell dinner
cooking, hug my wife hello, and spend the evening
telling her how much I love her. I'd like to go to bed
with her and not have to prove my virility, not have
to perform sexually beyond the call of duty, but just
give her love, and go to sleep knowing she'd be there
in the morning." (Joyce Lander, *Tough and Tender*).

George found out the hard way what the book of wisdom
told us thousands of years ago, "He who finds a wife finds a
good thing." (Proverbs 18:22). The grass is not greener on
the other side. If you have a wife you have a good thing. Let
her know it!

Praise Each Other

Out on the balcony of their treehouse which gave them

a breathtaking view of the lush jungle, Jane reminisces, "I used to worry about so many little things. But I learned not to worry as long as you are around. Wouldn't it be strange if I became as brave as you?" Jane asked. "Jane no need to be brave," Tarzan responds. "Jane beautiful. Jane good." He then lays a big kiss on her, sweeps her off her feet, and carries her into the treehouse for a rumble in the jungle.

Praise can come in all kinds of forms—words and deeds. One idea is to do an acrostic of each others name and do it in calligraphy or special print and frame it as a gift. Use your partners name as an acrostic to describe them. In Proverbs 31 it even speaks of praising our wives (and ladies, we should praise our husbands too). Praise builds up and wants to encourage your spouse to be a better person. Men, let God purify your motives in praising your wife. Mean it, and don't say it just as a means of obtaining sex. She will know whether you are for real anyway!

Money, mating and other matters that matter affect our relationships. If we look at each of these important areas with a willingness to change and improve, we can enhance our marriage.

Do you know the rhyme that says, "First comes love, then comes marriage, then comes _____ with a baby carriage"? Children and family usually follow mating. The next two chapters focus on the family aspect of our marriages. We pray they will help your marriage as you add children to your relationship.

CHAPTER 9

FAMILY TIES

In the movie, "Tarzan's New York Adventure," Boy (Tarzan and Jane's adopted son) gets kidnapped and taken to New York by a greedy American trying to make a big buck off Boy's ability to train elephants for circus tricks. Tarzan and Jane go to New York where they eventually end up in court in a custody dispute. Tarzan takes the stand to prove he is fit to be Boy's father.

His attorney asks, "What did you teach Boy?"

Tarzan replies, "Tarzan teach Boy where to find water when thirsty, how to find food when hungry. Tarzan teach Boy be strong like lion, be happy like bird."

The lawyer continues, "Do you find everything you need in the jungle?"

"Wise man need little."

"Have you thought what would become of Boy if he grows up in the jungle?" the lawyer continues.

Tarzan proudly states, "Boy grow up to be brother of sun, friend of rain. Hurt nobody, have nothing people have. Grow old like cedar tree. Boy will be good man, happy man."

The opposing lawyer begins his cross examination by asking, "Do you read, Tarzan?"

"Read?"

"Yes, read a book? Have you ever read Shakespeare's Hamlet?" the lawyer questions.

The King of the Jungle snaps, "Tarzan read trail in jungle. Read clouds in sky. Lawyer, ever hear of kenzanupa?

"Kenza what?" queried the lawyer.

"Kenzanupa cures snake bite. Every baby in jungle knows that." At this, the courtroom chuckles.

If we were on trial to prove if we were fit to be a father or parent, would we fare as well as Tarzan? Tarzan taught his son how to provide for himself, how to be content with what he had, to be strong as a lion but to be kind to others, to be good, and by being good, to be happy. The amazing thing is Tarzan could not read nor write, but the King of the Jungle taught Boy from his life experiences how to be the Prince of the Jungle. You don't need a formal education to teach your children. Our lives teach. Hopefully they teach our children how to be sons and daughters of King Jesus in the concrete jungle.

Kathy and I felt a couple chapters on family were essential to a book on marriage. One does affect the other. The family adds tension and stress, but it also brings us much joy and fulfillment and can strengthen us as couples.

The fabric of every society is the family. One of the greatest threats to our families is our fast-paced, entertainment-driven culture. Excessive running from one thing to another and filling our lives with movies and television erode the real sense of what it means to be a family. In fact, we are often strangers in the same house. When family members return home after a full day of activities, our schedules are often so varied that everyone eats individually rather than as a family. Afterwards we all proceed to watch TV until retiring to bed. Some families even watch their own programs separately as each child's room is equipped with a television. Does this sound familiar?

The reality is we have become individuals who happen to bear the same last name and live under the same roof, but that does not constitute a family. Knowing of the challenge before us to create real family time, we have dedicated this chapter to family ties. Along with our friends, Kathy and I will share our experiences, and in doing so, give you practical means to bond as a family

Family Reunions

It's important to see where you fit as a part of the family tree. Getting together with extended family helps family members to see there is something bigger they are connected to. Family should be important because it does give us a sense of belonging. Some families plan large reunions once a year or every several years. Other families, like ours, try to get together around Thanksgiving and Christmas time. It may be an elaborate dinner, an informal cookout or even a getaway at a lodge or resort. Gathering together reinforces the importance of extended family, and it fosters holiday traditions.

Deliberately building traditions into your family is important to strengthening the family ties. Here is an example of one family and their Thanksgiving tradition.

Shared by Lee and Alice, married 57 years

In 1969 we began having a family gathering around the Thanksgiving week. We have four grown children who all live in different parts of the country. Without these little reunions, we would not see each other possibly for several years. I love to exercise

109

and wanted my grandchildren to know its importance as well. Part of our tradition is to participate in the annual Turkey Trot held in our city. About 10 of the 16 grandchildren and some of my adult children join us for the run/walk of the three plus miles.

The rest of our time together is filled with great fun and fellowship. For example, as a former college basketball player I can still challenge the kids to a game of horse. Their interaction with one another is always special. Later the grandchildren ask questions of how their parents were as children. We reminisce on the past and catch up to where we are presently.

These special times rekindle the importance of both the immediate and the extended family. Many deep relationships have resulted among cousins, aunts, and uncles as a result of our time together. The joy and love we experience is precious and greatly cherished. I believe these reunions have deeply rooted my children's commitment to their marriages and family as a whole. These family times have played a factor in the fact that there has not been a divorce or separation in any of the marriages.

Mother/Daughter and Father/Son events

There are a number of events that give you opportunities to celebrate these relationships. A former Tampa Bay Buccaneer coach used to have an annual Father/Son day where fathers and their sons could come out to meet the players and hear them speak on the importance of family and the role their dads had in their lives. They also have a day where they encourage dads and their sons to camp out on the baseball field after watching the night game at

Tropicana Field with the Tampa Bay Devil Rays, a professional baseball team. There are usually many opportunities at church around Father's and Mother's Day to help bond the relationship (i.e. Mother/daughter banquet, Father/Son day, and special tea times).

Adopt a Family

Consider adopting a needy family. It might be a family whose dad is incarcerated or a single mom and her children who are struggling. Befriend them and seek to make a difference in their lives. It may mean giving them something you have materially, serving them in a special way, or being available to help out when you can. It can create a servant's heart in the children and also develop in them an appreciation for what they have as a family. It lets the children know that they have something to offer just by being who they are as a family. They can help, and even make a difference, in the lives of people who are not blessed with the same home life and the stability it offers.

Family Albums

Keep pictures of the journey together as a couple (i.e. pregnant wife, children's vacations, special events in each others lives, the big moves, etc.) My wife has also compiled a separate album for each child—with six children it's quite an effort in itself. Of course technology gives us the great opportunity to capture things on video, so a video library for the family is another way to frame the memories in time. Fond memories of the past can inspire hope that fuels our future together. And the albums make nice gifts for your children when they are grown with their own families. They can relive and tell their family about their childhood days, funny events, and share family traditions. Memories are important, not only the ones we cherish but also those painful ones that have made us into the people we are today.

Family Tree

Search out your family tree as a family. There are many companies online that can assist. You may find some interesting people, both the rogues and the righteous. It gives the family a sense of heritage and hopefully destiny. Perhaps they can see destiny's hand by finding who they are. It is also a fun discovery and adventure. One of the best software programs to assist you in finding the roots of your ancestors is Family Tree Maker. Go to www.myfamily.com. At present, the cost will be $50-100, depending on the database subscriptions you decide upon. The program makes the information obtained presentable with decorative charts, pictures and multimedia scrapbooks. You can save the information to a disk or publish it on a family web page.

Family Recipes

The holidays remind me of family recipes. We have special dishes that have been passed down from both sides of our parents. Some families go as far as to make a family recipe book and fill it with history of how great great Grandma used to do it and how you can fix that same meal today. For example, we have a special way to make kale, yellow rice, and chicken. Family recipes do not just pertain to holidays but also everyday meals that the kids can have fun learning how to make and carry on with their families.

Have a Garden

When we had a large piece of property in Texas, we planted our own garden. Each child had his own space and decided what to grow. Eventually everyone brought the fruit of their labor to the dinner table so we could all enjoy it and then boast of what a good job each child did.

There are many lessons about life that can come from gardening, such as understanding the process of time, the seasons of life, and the different conditions under which seeds will grow. These truths can teach children patience and give them the understanding that certain people will do better in different environments. It also helps them see the results of hard work.

Table Talk at Meal Times

Table talk puts a little structure to the family dinner time. Each person can bring a question or topic of discussion that the family can use as a stimulus for conversation. For example, as Christmas approaches, each family member can take their turn in telling about their most memorable one and why or what their favorite gift was. Around Thanksgiving, the children can take turns sharing why they are thankful.

Ronnie and Joanne give us their testimony on the subject of table talk.

Shared by Ronnie and Jo Anne, married 38 years

The one constant thing in our marriage of 38 years has been our insistence on having an evening meal together as a couple and family. It seems like a small thing, but when you have six children going many different directions, it is a major commitment. We both work and have had a ministry to the working poor, and it was a struggle to maintain this family evening tradition. We have been careful to keep that time together so that we can grow even closer. Even now with the kids grown, we still keep our schedule of an evening meal together. It has been the glue keeping us all connected and involved in each other's lives. We say the family that eats together, stays together. (There are stats proving how families that have meals together are more functional.) It has given us the opportunity to learn what one other did during their day and understand how we might help each other.

Funerals

When the death occurs of a family member who has had a very positive affect on the family and people around them, it is important to celebrate their profound influence at the funeral. A church marquee once read: "Live in such a way that the preacher won't have to lie at your funeral." This positive influence can be shared through many testimonies and pictures that bring back the fond memories of being together. This celebration reinforces the fact that we can have a positive influence on our family members and others.

When there has been no positive influence on us through the dead one's life, we can still use the funeral to draw close together to a scattered family and make commitments to love and be there for one another. It's a great time to make the commitment to communicate more often through e-mail, letters, cards, and even yearly visits if possible.

Game Nights

Turn off the TV and play cards, Yatzee, Monopoly, charades, or even games your family invents. When driving on a long trip, we play the alphabet game. This is a game you play using billboards and signs. As you travel, especially in

114

or near a city, look for words that begin with an alphabet letter. Start with A and proceed through the alphabet. Everyone helps find a word with the alphabet letter you are looking for. You see how fast you can go through the alphabet. (We fudge on X and Z sometimes and allow it to be in the middle of a word since they are difficult to find.)

As a general rule, the spirit of competition during games should not go from fun to fierce. The purpose of game nights is for family relationship building.

Kids in Training

Mothers need to train their daughters in taking care of the home: doing cooking, ironing, cleaning, and watching the smaller ones. The boys should not be left out either. Besides being taught to handle some of the outside chores, they need to learn how to handle domestic duties as well. These are roles that boys (someday men) might need to know and put to use. We tell our boys that someday they might be on their own, without a wife, and will need to know these skills. And it is quite nice to have a marriage where some of the domestic tasks can be shared. Kathy has been heard to say, "Remember, I'm not the maid." It is not the mom's responsibility to do all the household chores. As each helps in taking care of the home, it builds responsibility and a sense of a family unit.

Tell "Growing-Up" Stories

Tell your growing-up stories to your children. One of my kids' favorite things is to hear us share stories of when we were young. Tell them about the fun stuff—like when you got in trouble and how you were disciplined, or what their aunts or uncles were like growing up. They get a glimpse of events that shaped your life and how the things they go through in childhood will play an important part in shaping their lives. They also get a little history lesson of people, places, and events that brought you to where and who you are. Some of their favorite stories are telling them how my wife and I met, and the details of our dating and engagement. It is interesting to hear them tell the stories now because they can see the hand of God guiding their coming to existence. And these stories can be passed down to future generations.

A Family Pet

Tarzan and Jane were animal lovers in general. Yet, they had a pet. Remember cheetah? Of course, he was pretty self sufficient, no flea collars, shots, or spaying for him. Today having a pet is more complicated unless you too live in the jungle. The following story shares about having a family pet.

Pets can be a source of learning how to love, care, and take greater responsibility for another. Pets can make for some pretty special moments for the family. We had several pets, but one was most memorable. It was not the pet itself so much, but how we got it that we will never forget.

I had told my eldest daughter that there was no way we were going to get another pet; six children was enough. We were driving to Texas from Tampa, Florida, on a vacation. On the way we stopped at a friend's house in Pensacola. They had a cute little dog which I later found out is called a Lhasa Apso.

After being around the dog for a couple days, I told Leah, my oldest daughter, "If we ever get another dog, it will be like this one." Wrong thing to say! This dog was one of eight brothers and sisters that the owners were still trying to get rid of, and it turned out that they probably would give the dog for free if we wanted it. We agreed to look at the dog they had and if it was free, we would take it. Now the interesting part came when we spoke of getting a dog like theirs (our friends had a funny northeastern accent).

Our friend said, "Reggie has eight brothers and sisters who need a home." When he said Reggie (the name of the dog), it sounded like he said "Wedgie." I finally cleared it up privately when I questioned, "Your dog's name is Reggie, right?" He said, "Yes, Reggie" which sounded again like "Wedgie." Well, my kids heard it just as I had. When they got into the van they asked, "Dad, did he say the dog's name was Reggie or Wedgie?" Of course, I couldn't resist and I said, "Wedgie." "We will soon have our own Wedgie. In fact we will drive all the way back to Tampa with our Wedgie. There are seven other families that need one." Everyone started chiming in with their bit of wedge humor. "Dad, can our Wedgie have little wedges so we can sell them real cheap to families that always wanted their own wedgie but couldn't afford one?" "Dad, this means the family portrait will need to read, 'The Bernard Family and their Wedgie.'"

OK. I'll stop. The whole trip back and then some was filled with the Wedgie thing. A dog brought some memorable family moments for us. It can be a blessing to building family character and love.

Pets can also teach responsibility. The initial excitement of getting a pet can turn into negative complaints because it is not fun to feed and care for the pet. The novelty soon wears off and reality sets in in. Have you ever heard your child say, "I'll take care of it!" then a week later Mom is caring for the pet? Having a pet is not just a privilege but a responsibility. This is a vital lesson we can teach our children.

Build a Family Website

Many families have home computers that family members use frequently. An idea to build family relationships is to work on a family website together. You can create a secure family website with photos, e-mails and more through www.myfamily.com. The server can also function to locate members of your family tree. Allow each child to have their own page and add information about themselves that they feel is important.

You can chat exclusively online with other family members. It is also a great way to stay in touch with your spouse and children when the job, school, or marriage takes them away. Of course grandparents will love being able to know of family updates quickly, see photos of the growing kids, and be able to communicate more frequently.

The standard site is $29.95 and the super site is $109.95 per year. One of our children put some of our wedding photos on our site. I had no idea they had done it. Honoring our wedding and marriage in this way tells me of the hopes and expectations they have for their own.

Movie Night

Entertainment, like going to a movie, can be used to develop family time. After the movie, go and get ice cream or a pizza, giving time to discuss the movie. The conversation can move from simple likes and dislikes to deeper level sharing about moral and even political messages that the movie contained.

The other aspect of using entertainment in a positive light is to watch movies as a means of building a tradition or memories. Each year I watch "It's A Wonderful Life" with the family. It never gets old!

Honor Your Father and Mother

Honor your parents by planning to take care of them. As they provided for you in life, provide for them in the twilight years. It does not mean they cannot be in an assisted living facility, but it does mean that if they are there, then we still need to spend time with them. Making efforts to take care of them puts an intrinsic value on them that cannot be tarnished just because they are no longer in their productive years. How your children see you treat your parents are planting seeds for how they will treat you.

Families can be the source of so much happiness! The following chapter has more bits of practical parenting advice.

CHAPTER 10

MARRIED WITH CHILDREN

As if marriage or living with one person so different from you wasn't hard enough, then come the children. We have six. We finally figured out what was causing it. Yes, we got the TV fixed! Seriously, even though we never planned to have six children, we wouldn't do anything different. We haven't been perfect parents. In fact, at the writing of this book, one of our children has stopped actively living out her faith in God. There is an enemy out there called the devil whose devises are manifold in this world. Ultimately, our children make their own choices. We can protect them, guide them, influence them, but we cannot live for them.

The emotional, physical and financial demands of parenting can bring a marriage to the brink of disaster. What is most important is being on the same page as a couple with God and His Word.

Tarzan and Jane became parents instantly when they find a baby, whom they named Boy, in the jungle. To say the least it was a huge adjustment to their lives as they accept him into their family.

In watching the Tarzan movies that include Boy, you may also learn some things about what not to do regarding your children. For example, when Boy got into mischief nearly costing him his life and giving his parents agonizing concern, no discipline was administered—not even a time out from playing with the animals. Tarzan says to his son, "Boy, bad!" with a stern stare that immediately turns into a smile and a hug. This might get you by in an African jungle, but not in our temptation filled concrete jungle.

Use Proper Discipline

Many times our form of discipline for our children is a mirror of how we might have been disciplined when we were young. Instead of saying, "This is the way I was disciplined, so that's how I do it," we should ask, "How does God want me to discipline?"

It is extremely important that both parents have the same philosophy for discipline. If one is too strict and the other too loose in discipline, it leads to confusion for the child. Also, many times the child will go to the "loose" parent so they can get away with more things. Be in agreement and always ask, "Did you talk to Mom or Dad about this?" to see if they are using you against each other.

Decide on your mode of discipline. The kids do not need to see you fighting over how they will be disciplined. It is best to set the standard and tell them the consequences if they are broken ahead of time. This eliminates out of control anger.

Of course, one needs to discipline based on natural or rebellious actions. For example, if a child breaks a window by accident, the discipline is natural. They should help clean up the mess and maybe even pay for repairs. This does not warrant a spanking or grounding.

On the other hand, if a child talks back to you and tells you that he is not going to clean his room, this is a rebellious attitude. The scripture is quite clear what needs to be done with a rebellious child. Proverbs 13:24 says, "He who spares his rod hates his son, but he who loves him disciplines him diligently." Dealing with rebellion lets the child know who is in control. Children always want control and as parents we need to let them know that we are the ones in charge.

Our kids laugh now and say, "We remember when you would spank us and you would say, 'It's hurting me worse than it's hurting you.'" "Yeah, right," they would say. No parent wants to hurt their child. But sometimes we get confused that we will hurt them physically if we spank them. The scripture says we love them if we spank them. Why? We love them because we are protecting them from themselves. Kids want protection and control factors in their life. A spanking lasts a few minutes, but a rebellious attitude can last a lifetime and ruin a life.

I have found that putting control measures on this type of discipline is important and eliminates any false ideas of child abuse. First, talk to the child about what they did. Let them understand what they did is wrong and that is why they are being disciplined. Do not yell but calmly talk about it. If you are upset, send them to their room and allow some time for everyone to calm down.

Secondly, pray with them about their actions and use it as a time of repentance to God. Not only has your child sinned against you, but they have sinned against God.

Thirdly, tell them how many spankings they will get. Say, "I'm going to give you three spankings." If they buck the system, you can say, "I'll give you five spankings if you don't stop now." This helps you gauge your feelings and actions and eliminates exploding and spanking too much.

Fourthly, administer the punishment on the behind. I actually like using a rod, just as scripture mentions, as opposed to a belt or hand. I want them to know and see the rod as the instrument of correction and not my hands that I use for touching and loving them.

Lastly, allow a time for their crying and getting themselves under control. Then hold them close and reassure them of your love. You want to make sure your relationship is OK and your love is assured, although their actions were incorrect.

If you have been wrong in the way you have disciplined, you need to ask for your child's forgiveness. Do not add the "but" to your forgiveness. There are times when we blow it as parents. When we do, let's be big enough to acknowledge it and ask forgiveness. Our kids will love us more for it.

Unified Front

At a very early age, the children use tactics to manipulate you to get what they want. One of the oldest is to pit one parent against the other. Here is how it works. The child will ask mom if they can do something, and if they are denied, the child then goes to the father and asks him. I'm often preoccupied and say, "Yes, sounds good to me." An hour later, Kathy will ask me, "Where are the kids?" "Oh, I let them go play down the street," I'd say. Her reply reveals how the kids tried to manipulate us, "I told them they couldn't because they hadn't finished their chores."

The key to avoiding this problem is to always ask the child, "Have you asked your mother or father and what did she/he say?" It is important to be in agreement. You may not agree but you need to demonstrate unity in decision making or the children will know they can pit one parent against the other. If you do not agree, then talk it over privately and come to a decision that is unified. Raising children, especially in this information, entertainment age, is tough. When there are problems in the marriage, they are increased by the stress of dealing with our children.

Limit Arguing in Front of the Kids
Shared by Alan and Jule, married 15 years

As a rule, we try to limit our arguing in front of the children, but it does happen. We have found the biggest problem is not arguing in front of the children but leaving the conflict unresolved. If your children see the conflict, make sure they also see you resolve it and express love and respect afterwards. One day Alan and I had been arguing and then had to go somewhere in the car with our young son, Clark. At some point, Alan turned to me to apologize and I responded with my own apology. In the back seat we heard Clark softly say to himself, "My parents can work things out." We believe that we have given our children the gift of seeing that marriage, though difficult at times because of conflict, can be lovingly resolved. We don't always agree but we will always work things out. We hoped that we have prepared them with valuable skills in their own future marriages.

Children—Everyone Has an Assignment

For a household to properly function, it takes team work. Everyone needs to do their part. Building a healthy family means everyone understands they have a part to play. The key is defining those roles and their expectations. This also prepares children to play their role in the bigger society in which they will live. In my house there were few boy-ony and girl-only jobs; most were simply jobs. Different members were assigned tasks on various days, and there were consequences if they were not carried out.

Chores should be seen as a way to contribute to the family. Although we have given money on occasion for some types of chores, we do not normally pay our kids to do them. We should not use bribery to get something done. Sometimes we think that they cannot do the job so we just do it ourselves, but all ages can participate in chores. The problem is us. They certainly might not perform a task as well as we can do it, but it is a teaching experience and little by little they will improve. They need to be applauded for what they can do. Our four year old does chores and enjoys them. I give her chores that fit her capabilities—taking out cans for recycling, polishing tables, cleaning up her toys, and making her bed. Believe me, moms, you cannot do all of it by yourself. Create less stress in your life and allow everyone to pitch in!

Richard and Marge have nine children so giving each child an assignment isn't a luxury but rather a necessity. They tell us how they do it and give us other interesting details about their life as a large family.

Priorities in the Family
Shared by Richard and Marge, married 27 years

Life in our house is always exciting, filled with energy, activity, and noise. With nine children there is plenty to do. There are football games to attend, mountains of daily laundry and dishes to do, music lessons and projects to prepare for, and lots of visitors. On top of all this, the children are home schooled. So, how do we do it? There are five areas we emphasize in our family life every day: Devotions, priorities, team work, fun, and doing the "next thing." As we apply and do these five things we get things done.

Area 1: Devotions We begin everyday with a time of praise, worship, prayer and Bible reading. Everyone participates in playing a variety of musical instruments, and all pray for specific needs. This is

our most important family time as we put God first.
This time of devotions carries over into everything
else we do during the day.

Area 2: Priorities Life is too fast, full, and dis-
tracting to neglect setting priorities. Most families do
not even eat together. Setting the right priorities requires us to determine what is most important and
pleasing to God and then planning around those
things. Prioritizing our family life means we must
learn to say no to many things so as not to strain the
whole family. Family time together is more important than individual accomplishment or activities.
One easy way to insure that family time is not ne-
glected is to eat meals together. Plan your schedule
around meal times as much as possible.

Area 3: Teamwork We could not accomplish the
many things we do without a team effort. Each child
has a "buddy"—an older child is paired with a
younger one. The older child helps the younger one
with chores, school work, and anything else the
younger one needs help with. Every child participates in chores. They help prepare meals, set and
clear the table, do dishes, clean the kitchen, bath-
rooms, and pick up their bedrooms. Each child has a
special day every week in which they do not have to
do their assigned chores. On their day, they also lead
the family in prayer over the meal.

Area 4: Fun Laughter and love make a house a
home and turn dreary tasks into exciting adventures.
Even doing dishes can be fun when we all pull together and talk, joke, sing, tell stories, and play
harmless pranks. Children want to be with their parents and siblings when the focus is on fun. Having
fun means we enjoy being together. It creates a safe

environment of love and acceptance for children and relieves them of fear and insecurity.

Area 5: Doing the next thing Finally, there are times when life gets crazy. Unexpected things happen—sickness, visitors, or projects. What do we do when things get too full or tense? We just do the "next thing." Instead of panicking or getting stressed over uncontrollable intrusions or problems, we have learned to focus on the things we can do and especially to take those things one at a time. Life is today, at this moment. We cannot allow worry over what might happen tomorrow rob us of the precious moments we have right now.

Keep a Journal for Your Kids

I have kept a journal for each child. Daniel and I have taken the opportunity to write to our kids just what we saw in them and how God was speaking to us about them. We hope they will go back and read these after they become adults and treasure their life growing up. It is nice to start this journal even before the child is born to communicate your heart and thoughts. As events, milestones, sayings, or ideas/reflections come to you, write them down. The journal does not have to only include the parent's words but also grandparents and other people who are significant to the family can participate. Write about values, dreams, prayers, and daily events.

Part of the birthing process is to give the child a name. It is more meaningful if both parents are involved in the process. A friend of ours took the meaning of our children's first and middle names and, using calligraphy, artfully wrote the names and their meaning and framed them. We have used the meaning of our children's name to speak into their lives just to affirm they are unique and God has a special plan for them.

⸱ Plan the Family Date

My children need more one-on-one time with me than they need more toys. It took discipline and I had to work at it, but I have monthly "whatever you want to do" dates with them. These are individual dates with each child to communicate to them my love and their value to me. All work and no play made me a dull and distant dad and husband. Working at making my wife and family as my main priority is a lesson I learned well. It takes time and effort to plan and budget for the vacation or make reservations for a restaurant to make sure your evening is not spoiled with a long wait. It is special efforts like that which make the difference and says to your family, "You're what's important to me."

Aspire to have a strong physical presence with your children. If both spouses work, take turns watching them. A child needs both parents to speak into their lives. If you are a single parent, of course, it is much more difficult. In this case you will have to prioritize. Sometimes you can either work late and earn some extra money or spend extra time with your child. You can commit to more church activities or you can have family time. If you are pushing your children aside and rationalizing your actions, you show them they are not important.

The Birds and the Bees

It is very important to communicate to our children about their sexuality, where babies come from, and the benefits of staying chaste for your life partner. God designed these things to be taught within the confines of the family and not by their 6th grade teacher. I can see why the school system feels it's their job to do because so many parents are abdicating their responsibility in this area.

We need to talk to our children on a truly honest and positive level about sex. We need to let them know why God created different sexes, and we need to give them accurate information about the reproduction process. There are many good books on this subject geared for different ages. An excellent series to instruct our children in this area is the *God's Design for Sex* children's book series put out by Navpress. Their books break down information by ages: 3-5; 5-8; 8-11; 11-14. Check your local Christian bookstore for additional resources.Take the time to give your children the right information. They might act in an inappropriate way on the information they receive from their peers or even teachers.

It's important to teach our children how to relate and respect those of the opposite sex. Of course, we demonstrate that respect best within our marriage. We need to teach a boy how to properly treat a young lady, and a girl how to properly respond to a young man.

Dealing With Teenagers

The teen years can tear a family apart, add stress that puts years on your life span, or be some of the best and most memorable years with your children. All you need is one rebellious teen to know you don't want to go there again. Pick the right battles to win the war. There are areas of compromise that you and your wife must agree upon such as hair color and style. The battles you need to win in order to win the war are those things which you can't compromise because in the end they compromise the growth and well being of your child. Another way to put it is you need to major on the majors and not on the minors.

1. Be Involved

Ask questions, a lot of them: Who are your friends? Where are you going? Who are you going with? and How long will you be? They probably will hate it, but it's necessary. If something happened to them it would haunt you forever wondering why you weren't more involved in their lives. Friends are an important component to their lives so it is necessary that you have input into them. The two teens that shot and killed their fellow students at Columbine High didn't have involved parents asking questions.

2. Enforce Rules

Keeping curfews and having consequences when the guidelines are violated are important. If they don't understand keeping rules and the consequences for not staying within their framework, they will be ill prepared for the rules of living in the world. The rules are merely guidelines to having the best relationship with those in authority over them and with others (siblings) they live with. A household where everyone is doing their own thing will always be a house but never a home.

My parents never put restrictions on me in my teen years. My dad was a heavy drinker and he probably felt he wasn't a good example to be able to give too much discipline. I always wondered why they did not discipline me or give me some guidelines to adhere to.

3. Keep Them in the Word

If you are a Christian parent, you want to instill godly character and principles into your children's lives. This is done by keeping them in the Word in a variety of ways. Family devotions are a great way to do it collectively. This can be a great teaching time so they will come to understand what they are reading.

For the younger child, reading Bible stories and books to

them is important. You are creating an attitude of importance to them. If something is important, you spend time doing it. I remember when one of our daughters, Faith, read through her entire Children's Bible when she was quite young. She was proud of her accomplishments.

Kids also need to see you reading the Word and applying it. As they get older, they need to take on the responsibility of spending more personal time with God. This happens gradually until they have a personal relationship of their own with God. Our goal is that they can read the Word and seek God for themselves.

It is important that as a parent you stress their having a quiet time, one-on-one with God. If you were to ask any of my kids what are three things that I stress need to be done everyday before their time for T.V., computer, etc., they would quickly chime in—quiet time, chore(s) and homework. And, as was already mentioned, all of these areas develop responsibility to God, their family, and their school.

4. Develop a College or Training Fund

College and technical training is getting more expensive by the day. Creating a college savings fund, where you can often lock into today's college prices even though they will not be attending for another 15 years can take off the stress and pressure when those college days arrive. If such a program is not available in your state, begin to save through other means. Seek out a financial advisor. Today we need Christians in every facet of society living out their faith. In my opinion, everyone is called to full-time ministry. The vocation or business God leads you to be is your vehicle for that ministry assignment. With this in mind, we need to think of securing the best training and job preparation for them as possible. The goal is to excel in what we do in order to give glory to God and a witness to the world around us.

Feeling Like a Failure

"Kathy, I don't think I can love another child as much as I love this one..." These were my words concerning our first born. We gave her so much attention even before she was born. We prayed, talked, and read scriptures to her while she was in the womb. Did we make mistakes? Yes, like all new parents, we made our share of mistakes, but we tried to be consistent in our love and discipline.

Although our daughter was trained from birth to love God and have a relationship with Him, she has not chosen to continue that relationship at this time. Where did we go wrong? Many times we have said, "We should have done this or that." Countless times we have second-guessed ourselves, and our 20/20 hindsight seems so much clearer. However, we realize more than ever that:

Everyone has the freedom of choice. She began making choices when she was twelve. We stand in prayer daily for her to come into her God-given destiny. We forgive ourselves and we forgive her for the hurts. We trust that God's Word will not return void but accomplish that which He desires. She has read God's Word during all her growing up years. She still quotes it to her unsaved friends when religious topics arise.We have hope that she will change just as Billy Graham's son, Franklin, did. He was a rebel until he came back to the Lord when he was 32 years old.

We are humbled more than ever to follow God's path. We wanted the picture perfect family, but that is still in development. We are not giving up. God is bigger than our mistakes and our daughter's mistakes. His love continues to surround her even though she doesn't recognize or acknowledge it. Don't give up hope! Keep fighting for your prodigal son or daughter.

CHAPTER 11

NEW BEGINNINGS

We pray these real life examples, bits of wisdom, and creative ideas we have included have been an encouragement to you as a couple. Again, it is not always the big thing but rather the little things we do that make the difference.

Let us know what has worked for you in this book. Submit your own creative and unique approach to a problem you faced or a fresh idea so we can share it with others. Go to www.marriagesthatwork.com to submit what has worked for you. Additional helps and testimonials can be found through the site.

Anything of value takes work. Your marriage is valuable in the sight of God, to your family members, and to society; and it is worthy of your best effort. Have a plan of action. Make some goals and set short-term dates to keep yourselves accountable and on course. For instance, you might decide to write two notes of encouragement a week and have a special date night once a week to improve communication and intimacy in your marriage. Evaluate yourselves after a month. If the changes are something that works for you, continue making them an habitual part of your life. Once you have success in that area, you can look for another way to deepen your relationship. Hopefully you will be able to look back after a year and see real progress. This progress will use the fuel called faith and encouragement to help you continue working on your marriage.

The most rewarding, fulfilling, and blissful life a person can have on earth is by sharing it with your lifetime marriage partner. Our prayer for each of your relationships comes from Numbers 9:6: "May God keep you and bless you (and your marriage). May He cause His face to shine on your relationship."

You can beat the odds and make your marriage work. With commitment, determination, and daily attention, your marriage will not only work but be a testimony to others who are struggling to make their marriage work.

Our hope is that this book has served to encourage you to try some new things. This, if nothing else, will make your marriage like that of our jungle duo—a real adventure! A workbook can be downloaded from our website www.MeTarzanYouJane.net to help you become more intentional in areas that could use some work. We'd like to hear from you to know how you are doing or if you have an idea that has worked. Drop us a line at the address below.

Just like the story of Tarzan and Jane, your relationship can stand the test of time. Like them, you too can cultivate a lasting relationship that is not just on "survival mode" but on its way to becoming a modern-day classic.

———•———

To contact the authors, write or call:
Daniel and Kathy Bernard
P.O. Box 4486, Clearwater, FL 33758
www.sctb.org • 727-536-2273
Daniel@sctb.org